What people are saying about …

# THE DRO▮

"In the self-centered, *me first* world we live in, it ▮▮▮ ▮▮ly amazing to see a man giving his life for the sake of children who had no hope, and also to see the young filmmaker whose life was changed forever by witnessing it. This book is emotional and profound in every way. Stop what you are doing and read on."

**Jon Erwin,** writer and director of *October Baby* and *Woodlawn*

"Brian Ivie bids us to come gather round his campfire and listen to a story … not about him, or Pastor Lee—but about us. It's an illuminating, inspiring, warm, penetrating fire, magical and mysterious. He is not the light; he has found a way to share the light he's been given. And he asks each of us to put something of ourselves into the flames. *The Drop Box* is a great story, well-told by a gifted storyteller and friend."

**John Shepherd,** executive producer of
*Man Down* and *The Ultimate Gift*

"Lisa and I were deeply touched when we watched *The Drop Box*. We live in a culture that makes heroes of the wrong people. [This story] exposes us to a true hero and a worthy example to follow."

**Francis Chan,** bestselling author of *Crazy Love* and *Forgotten God*

"*The Drop Box* tells a moving story of God's subversive, selfless, fatherly love undercutting selfishness, saving the unwanted, and transforming lives in unpredictable ways and surprising places."

**Barnabas Piper,** author of *The Pastor's Kid*
and the forthcoming *Help My Unbelief*

"This young man is a game changer. I encourage you to read this powerful life-changing story. This is the kind of book we need to get into the hands of the next generation!"

**Michael Catt,** author of *Courageous Living* and
lead pastor of Sherwood Church, Atlanta

"Brian Ivie brings a compelling story together through wit and honesty that never fails to connect. This book is a great resource for anyone earnest about living a life on mission for Christ."

**Will Bakke,** writer and director of *Beware of Christians* and *Believe Me*

"What a stimulating story! Brian Ivie shares his journey with remarkable honesty and refreshing humor. Reading his story put a smile on my face and hope in my heart. It was such a joy to see how God captured the heart of this filmmaker. Those who love movies will especially enjoy his narrative. Read it and enjoy the journey."

**Rev. Sammy Tippit,** author of *God's Secret Agent* and *Twice a Slave*

"I love seeing God raise up young artists to put His glory on display through their creativity. Brian's riveting story magnifies the reality that God has created each of us in His image for something much bigger than a pension and a mortgage. I was gripped by the vivid story and captivated by Brian's vast knowledge of film. He writes like a man on a mission, and I want to join it with him! Read this, be moved, and follow the same Jesus on His path for you."

**Alvin L. Reid, PhD,** professor of evangelism and student ministry, Southeastern Baptist Theological Seminary

"*The Drop Box* is the kind of book we all need to encounter from time to time, to sort of reboot the way we look at the people around us. Reminders of the depravity of mankind are best served like this, as appetizers for a celebration of the Redemption we have in Christ and how he continues to work through broken vessels to bring his love and mercy to every corner of this sin-cursed world. This could easily have been a book that made the reader feel helpless and insignificant in light of such an overwhelming endeavor of love; instead, it inspires us as we follow the author on a journey from San Clemente to Seoul to Sundance, to find God working in the most unexpected places, and to sacrifice our idols—trading them for a cross."

**Zachary Bartels,** author of *The Last Con* and *Playing Saint*

"Brian Ivie makes an award-winning film and now gives us a humorous and honest look inside the mind of a young filmmaker. Compelling prose about his journey of faith and straight talk about his life, loves, and losses. An artistic insightful read, rich with candor and comedy."

**David I. Levy, MD,** author of *Gray Matter: A Neurosurgeon Discovers the Power of Prayer … One Patient at a Time*

"In *The Drop Box*, author and filmmaker Brian Ivie brilliantly tells not only the story of how one man's passion is saving the lives of unwanted babies on the streets of Seoul, South Korea, but how Brian himself was led to redemption through the life and testimony of this man. If you are looking for a riveting story that will challenge you to live a life of deeper purpose and meaning, then *The Drop Box* is the book for you."

**Adam Stadtmiller,** author of *Praying for Your Elephant*

"*The Drop Box* is a story of a director showing the world what grace looks like. That grace is powerful because it changes the lives of all who encounter it. But the director of this story is God. And He shows us what His grace looks like in the heart of Pastor Lee and through the lives of these precious children. No one who encounters this grace can ever be the same again. Brian's life was changed by this story. My life was changed by this story. Your life will be changed as you discover this story is also your story—a child saved by a Father's love."

**Eddie Byun,** author of *Justice Awakening: How You and Your Church Can Help End Human Trafficking*

"*The Drop Box* is a raw, unadulterated journey of one person's life—or so it might seem. For I truly believe that as you ingest its pages, you may discover it's your story as well. And my hope is that in reading *The Drop Box*, you might be delivered from whatever it is that holds you. Brian's willingness to be transparent with himself forced me to take a good hard look at myself. Expect to self-reflect. Expect to be challenged. Expect to be changed. For the message of God's incredible love radiates from its pages."

**Dr. Keith Loy,** lead pastor of Celebrate Community Church, Sioux Falls

"The lines of reality and art get crossed as Brian searches for truth and hope in a world that offers little of each. Brilliantly written and laced with humor, Brian tells a story that humanity is hungry to hear—satisfaction is possible and all of life matters to someone, even yours."

**Drew Sodestrom,** lead pastor of Vintage Grace Church, Sacramento

"In a world that is obsessed with pretending everything is fine, *The Drop Box* is a breath of fresh air. Brian Ivie deals candidly with the darkness that has plagued his heart, and this makes his ecstasy in the hope he discovered real and inspiring. It is at once a commentary on the human condition and a wonderful journey into the foibles of a filmmaking college student who got in way over his head. Honest, intelligent, and convicting; this is what a good memoir looks like."

**W. A. Fulkerson,** author of the Starfall trilogy

"When I picked this book up I expected it to read like so many others before it: a conversion experience against the backdrop of an unbelievable story of sacrifice and triumph (essentially, a story where you couldn't help but be converted). But what I found was so much more. So much more real, and so much more relatable. This is a story about the lie of the American (and Korean) dream. It's a story about suburbia, being numbed to death by the trappings of comfort and material. It's about the failures of our parents and the sovereignty of God to use extraordinary circumstances to reveal His truth in the midst of the numbing malaise that is everyday Americana. In the end, this book is about adoption. It is one of the single greatest illustrations and expressions of the Father's willingness to take us home. To take us where we belong."

**Rev. Benjamin J. Roby,** pastor of Heritage Baptist Church

# THE DROP BOX

HOW 500 ABANDONED BABIES,
AN ACT OF COMPASSION,
AND A MOVIE
CHANGED MY LIFE FOREVER

# BRIAN IVIE
## WITH TED KLUCK

David C Cook
*transforming lives together*

THE DROP BOX
Published by David C Cook
4050 Lee Vance View
Colorado Springs, CO 80918 U.S.A.

David C Cook Distribution Canada
55 Woodslee Avenue, Paris, Ontario, Canada N3L 3E5

David C Cook U.K., Kingsway Communications
Eastbourne, East Sussex BN23 6NT, England

The graphic circle C logo is a registered trademark of David C Cook.

Scripture quotations marked NIV are taken from the Holy Bible, New
International Version®, NIV®. Copyright © 1973, 2011 by Biblica, Inc.™ Used
by permission of Zondervan. All rights reserved worldwide. www.zondervan.
com. Scripture quotations marked ESV are taken from The Holy Bible, English
Standard Version® (ESV®), copyright © 2001 by Crossway, a publishing
ministry of Good News Publishers. Used by permission. All rights reserved.

Some names have been changed to protect individuals and their stories.

LCCN 2014957683
ISBN 978-0-7814-1306-0
eISBN 978-0-7814-1327-5

© 2015 Brian Ivie and Ted Kluck

The Team: Andrew Stoddard, Nick Lee, Tiffany Thomas, Karen Athen
Cover Design: Amy Konyndyk
Cover Photos: Alice Lee and Paul Youn

Printed in the United States of America
First Edition 2015

2 3 4 5 6 7 8 9 10

042015

# CONTENTS

# ACKNOWLEDGMENTS

## FROM TED

When I started this project, I didn't know Brian Ivie. However, shortly after connecting, I received a package in the mail containing various artifacts from his life and trips to South Korea—ticket stubs, sketches, note pads, video clips, and even a children's book entitled *Just Me and My Dad*. And what's cool is that what he sent didn't necessarily portray him in the most amazing light possible, as is often the case with ghostwriters' clients. Soon we were talking about movies, busting each other's chops via text, and basically doing the things friends do.

We talked a few times each week to "interview," but often the interviews turned into discussions about our fathers, discussions about movies, and discussions about business, which in my opinion are the best possible interviews (the ones that don't sound like interviews). Sometimes he would put me on the phone with whoever was in his office at the moment. Best of all was Brian's commitment to praying before each session—a process that helped me tremendously, as I remembered why we were doing this in the first place: to bring honor and glory to our heavenly Father.

So thank you, Brian, for being authentic (that's an overused and trite-sounding word, but still) and fun. You still remind me of the Jason Schwartzman character in *Rushmore*.

Thanks as well to my good friend and agent, Andrew Wolgemuth, for having integrity, having a personality, and caring about more than just the bottom line. You are the best at what you do.

Thanks to our editorial team at David C Cook for taking this project on short notice and for being as excited about it as we are.

Thank you to Pastor Lee for listening to the Holy Spirit's prompting and for losing your life to save children. Thank you to both of the women, whom I've never met, who put our sons up for adoption many years ago in Ukraine. You made a courageous choice, and I'm so grateful to care for your boys now.

And finally, thank you to both my earthly father and my heavenly Father. Brian and I wanted to write this book as sons, in such a way as to honor our fathers. Thank You, Lord, for new hearts, for forgiveness, and for the chance to be Your adopted sons.

## FROM BRIAN

After sharing my testimony at tons of small, out-of-the-way churches, people often told me I should make a movie about making the movie. Basically, a glorified behind-the-scenes featurette on my life and coming to faith while creating *The Drop Box* in South Korea.

I was always humbled by that idea but also thought it sounded really conceited and vain. Instead, I've decided to write a lengthy memoir.

First, thanks must go to Ted Kluck, my ghostwriter and shrink, who wanted to write a good story that was bigger than me. After that, I want to shout out to Andrew Wolgemuth and RJ Moeller, who made sure that we found the right publishing home, and then of course to Andrew Stoddard, Tiffany Thomas, and the entire David C Cook team, who had the heart from the very beginning.

Thank you to my uncle Keith Tanabe for being an example of sacrifice; my aunt Christine DiGiacomo for praying for me since I was born; and my manager, Dave Mechem, for keeping me on course and thinking my stories are worth telling.

Thanks as well to my spiritual parents, Rob and Patrice, for "adopting me" and showing me how to walk as a beloved son.

Thank you to Sarah Choi for being the sister I never had and for pouring out your heart for these lost children in an unparalleled way. Thank you to Shayan Ebrahim for going back to South Korea with me and for being a true friend in the toughest times. Thank you to Todd Burns and Bud Keilani for protecting the movie and for living out the tender heart of the Father. Thank you to Wes Fulkerson for being as true and steadfast as Barnabas was for Paul. And thank you to Andy Kim, Jen Alt, Staci Brown, and JC Park for building Kindred Image into an organization that loves people eternally.

Thank you to Sam Jo, Sterling Phillips, Jin Doo, Tavis Robertson, and Mitch McDuff for going on the first adventure with me and for never giving up, even when I did.

A big thanks to Mark Thomas for constantly challenging my faith, to David Beylik for teaching me about grace in the most unforgettable way, and to Bryce Komae for showing me what real joy and real freedom look like.

Thank you also to Will Tober, the guy who led me to Christ and who remains the person with a heart most like God's in my life.

Thanks of course to my baby brother, Kevin Ivie, for being a hilarious and heartfelt friend.

And thank you to my amazing mother, Tomi Ivie, for going outside of herself every single day to raise a complicated guy like me.

Thank you to my fiancée, and soon-to-be amazing wife, Amanda Borland, for loving me after knowing the worst about me.

But in the end, this book is for my dad, William Carey Ivie, the man who carried me in a pouch on his back when I was little, and still does in many other ways.

## Introduction

# ALL THE WAY HOME

*In the future, everybody is going to be a director. Somebody's got
to live a real life so we have something to make a movie about.*

Cameron Crowe

When I was flying back home from South Korea last July, the
plane started to shake. It started to shake so much that the flight
attendants looked concerned. That's how you know it's bad. When
the flight attendants stop smiling and look for open seats in the
cabin. I remember I was sitting next to a guy named Griffin, who
had just married someone he really loved. After shooting the
breeze for ten to fifteen, I told him the story that I tell in this
book. The one about the box and the babies and the boy who got
saved.

   Ever since my first trip to South Korea back in 2011, I've told
that story to almost every single person I've sat next to. Every
time I travel, I plop down against the window, pop in my white
Apple earbuds, and try to gather the courage to unplug myself
and unpack the miracles that led me there.

As my friend Mark Thomas once told me, "Airplanes are the best place to win souls, man. Where are they going to run?"

With Mark's admonition rattling around in my mind, I usually start with something like, "You come here often?"

Just kidding.

More like, "So, how was your trip?"

Pretty harmless.

Most people are actually really up for talking, at least the people God puts next to me. And don't get me wrong, I really enjoy telling my story, but many times people end up telling me their stories too. I even sat next to this lady whose nephew had overdosed literally right before she got on the plane. She closed her cell before scooting past me, and I could see in her face that someone had died. Carol carried her nephew's death between her teeth. But I could also see the faraway daze of someone who had to sit normally for six hours before doing anything about it.

She still had to fly, pick a soda from the trolley, wear her seat belt when the light went on, and wait for her black bag to come around the carousel. And that wasn't the only bag she would see that day.

So I talked to Carol for six hours about God.

All the way home.

Growing up in Orange County all my life, I'd never really known a lot about death, or even about pain. My best friend never died in a car wreck, my dad never missed a local Triathlon, and my healthy

Asian mom still buys me food from Costco when I come home for the weekend. But sitting next to Griffin, pinned against the window of a creaky airbus, I'd be lying if I said I wasn't holding something between my teeth.

Griffin listened as I spun the usual yarn. I felt like his grandfather telling him about the Korean War or something. It was cool how he listened. After that, he told me how he grew up, went to church, slept around, felt sorry, went to church, slept around, and started the cycle all over again. It was an authentic conversation, full of expletives. That's how you know someone isn't turned off by your God story: when they still use curse words around you afterward.

In between stories, the plane started shuddering violently again. Griffin seemed to like the bumps, kind of like John Candy liked driving against traffic in *Planes, Trains, and Automobiles*. Hair standing and knuckles white, I asked my new friend if planes could fall just from turbulence. He just tipped back his whole beer and said, "I don't think so."

It was about that time that I considered ordering some whiskey, and I hate whiskey. Then, like I had jinxed it, the plane literally dropped out of the air. I mean plummeted like Lex Luthor's Drop Of Doom at Six Flags Magic Mountain. The whole cabin yelled to high heaven, except Griffin and me. I wanted to scream, but I was the Christian, so I tried to show Griff that I wasn't afraid. My new friend was sauced, but I'm sure he could still tell that this wasn't exactly coming up roses.

Truth was, we needed God, or Liam Neeson, or Samuel L. Jackson. And we needed him soon.

A few seconds later, the plane caught itself, or maybe God caught it, I don't know. It was a good thing I had eleven more hours of flight time so I could consider the possibilities. From that point forward, Griffin and I both went into our own worlds. He watched some Korean action flick and I watched some American action flick. That's what film snobs do, by the way, when they're flying international. They watch the movies they'd otherwise make fun of.

At least that's me anyway.

In the movie *Flight*, directed by Robert Zemeckis, Denzel Washington flies a plane upside down through the spire of a KKK church before crash-landing and waking up in the hospital, where John Goodman later shows up with a ponytail and lots of drugs. If you haven't seen it and that little description doesn't hook you, I don't know what else to do here. But it's safe to say that I had considered how our Delta flight might do the same. How we might go down like Denzel and at least take some evildoers down with us in a whirl of glory. What I learned after seeing that movie, though, is that there's actually a legal term for those instances when something happens outside of human control. Like a plane crash.

Lawyers call it an "Act of God." Seriously, that's the legal language for it.

Google defines it this way: "An instance of uncontrollable natural forces in operation (often used in insurance claims)."

I spent several hours thinking about how epic it would be to go out in an "Act of God," or how terrifying.

But the very first time I flew to South Korea, two years before, I didn't have a story for the guy or girl in the middle seat. I didn't have a story about God.

Because back in December 2011, as I flew six thousand miles to make a movie about saving Korean babies, I had no idea God was planning to save me.

Chapter 1

---

# KIDS TEAMING UP
# AGAINST EVIL

*I never had any friends later on like the ones I*
*had when I was twelve … does anyone?*

Gordie, *Stand by Me*

I have wanted to make movies since I was nine.

Much like the recent Ben Affleck, I would act in and direct my own projects. One day, it would be great to sit around a director's roundtable and swap stories with Ben. He could fill me in on the travails of shooting little films like *Argo* or *The Town,* and I could delight him with how I staged ambitious battle scenes for *The Lord of the Rings* (Part 4) behind my house.

I couldn't articulate it at the time, but my favorite movies as a kid always centered on the idea of kids teaming up against evil. *The Goonies, 3 Ninjas,* and *The Sandlot* were my staple rentals from Hollywood Video before "the Man" shut it down to build strip clubs and other childhood-crushing hovels. I was always more drawn to movies where kids would ride their BMX bikes into town and find an abandoned treasure map than movies where British schoolkids would reckon with talking beavers (*The Chronicles of Narnia*). I wanted to watch something that could actually happen to me.

Something that I could actually find "behind my house."

At the same time, when I made movies, I wanted to be in a battle, because being in a battle is how you became heroic. And also because everything around me—affluent suburbia—was the diametric opposite of a battle. To me, there were no heroes in Orange County. Just a lot of bored people with broccoli wads of cash.

When I started making my childhood movies, I would invite over the kids who looked most like trolls or elves and hand them lines from *The Fellowship of the Ring*. Typecasting began early for me. Later in my career, I would cast my brother as James Bond in my original film, *James Bond*. I never had a script, but always came up with lines on the spot. I liked finding the story in the wild and got electrified by the process of coming up with twists and turns in a plot that even I didn't see coming. That's how I still make movies, I think.

My process was a little frustrating for whomever was there helping, but most kids showed up for the sword-fighting parts anyway, so they usually let me dream.

Unlike going to school, making movies kept me awake. That's the best way to explain it. When I held a camera in my hands, I didn't need to eat or even sleep. Every day was Christmas Eve, and I burned with anticipation and wide-eyed wonder.

Every summer, I would knock on doors and wrangle the neighborhood kids together to make one of these movies. Sometimes we'd make them during a single sleepover, in between barbaric video game rounds of *GoldenEye* or *Super Smash*. Other times we'd work for weeks on end. Then one fateful day Taylor Abramson got a real camera. I'm talking top-of-the-line prosumer stuff, the stuff dreams are made of. I knew we were finally ready to shoot something dramatic, something gutsy, something us.

So, in true form, I got all the kids together to stage yet another version of *The Fellowship of the Ring*.

This time, however, the battles were bigger, Taylor and I started adding our own original characters, and we even put together the cash to buy a Howard Shore CD. During shooting, we blasted the original *LOTR* music and dressed up the older kids in *Scream* costumes from the dollar store because that's the closest we could get to Ringwraiths. We even cleverly inverted the footage when I (Frodo) wore "the one ring to rule them all" to show off our iMovie VFX chops, and hired a thirteen-year-old hockey player from the end of the cul-de-sac to be our stunt coordinator.

This is what you do before you like girls.

The thing about making movies before you like girls, of course, is that there aren't any girls in the movie. You end up with an all-male ensemble (hence, *LOTR*) and skip the kissing parts. The big benefit, though, is that you're free to find inventive ways of killing everyone in the movie, since it's "just the guys." I'll never forget when this kid named Jacob from up the street leaped over a large rock (my futon) and slammed Collin in the neck with a plastic devil's fork when we entered "The Mines of Moria" (my garage). When I look back, everything I made seems like some kiddy iteration of *Final Destination*. Anyway, our parents were proud of us. So proud, in fact, that my buddy Evan's dad even helped us edit it all together and set up a screening with every family in the neighborhood.

My parents didn't know it then, but I was planning to make this circus the rest of my life.

□

Over the years, kids filtered in and out of my little Hollywood. It had become clear that we enjoyed paying homage to three movies and three movies only, so my mom bought plastic bins to keep all the costumes and props so that we could efficiently mount the same productions all over again every summer. The structure of these films went more or less like this:

### THE LORD OF THE RINGS

Scene 1: Gandalf hands out weapons, plus all relevant exposition (i.e., evil everywhere, get busy)

Scene 2: Traveling montage

Scene 3: Dramatic Orc ambush, supporting character dies horribly

Scene 4: Final battle near local playground, featuring a slow-motion sword fight with "the boss"

Scene 5: Create huge expectations for a sequel

### JAMES BOND

Scene 1: Slow-motion walk to "Apache" by The Sugarhill Gang

Scene 2: Instead of a Bond girl, we meet some physically inferior male counterpart

Scene 3: Tongue-in-cheek training montage

Scene 4: Gadget-choosing scene and/or car chase

Scene 5: International spy ring thwarted

## HARRY POTTER

Scene 1: Harry Potter's scar is shown (clearly washable marker)

Scene 2: Dudley tries not to break character while wearing a couch pillow under his sweater to make him look fat

Scene 3: We throw thousands of empty letters (more like fifty) that we've borrowed from Evan's dad's office from the banister

Scene 4: We realize at this point that we'll need both someone to play Hermione and a large castle

Scene 5: We use all available monies to shoot *The Lord of the Rings* again

In the end, none of this was really about the end product to me. When it all started, I never really thought about making movies in real life. Truth be told, I just wanted to stab the bad guys (more pillows under their shirts), lift candleholders from my parents' dining room set, and find myself in a deadly ambush alongside my best friends. We led our warring factions together because inside of us was a desire to see pure innocence battle pure evil. But I think there's something in every boy that longs for that. Something that longs to defeat evil.

Even before we know there's evil in our own hearts.

□

When I was fifteen, my dad drove us to Turlock, California (his hometown), to begin my first foray into semi-original work. The movie was called *Sierra Street* and starred me, my brother, and my friends. Much to the production accountant's dismay (my dad again) it was also a major period piece set in the 1950s, which is inarguably the greatest kids-teaming-up-against-evil era of all. You knew it was set in the fifties because the song "Lollipop" played in the beginning and also because one of the characters wore a Davy Crockett coonskin hat. I appeared to weigh about eighty-three pounds when we filmed Sierra Street. In addition to the Crockett hat, the film also had:

- The obligatory kid with thick nerd glasses (my neighbor John)
- A creepy old man (my grandpa)

- A retro-looking brick high school
- A dark, shadowy hand coming out from a dark corner and covering a kid's mouth
- Still no females at all, not even in the background

The only things we were missing were a good microphone, lighting equipment, an appropriate crew, period props, period costumes, music licenses, and legal rights to the source material.

Hey, it was a kid movie.

I did, however, direct and star.

Despite the fact that *Sierra Street* was made by the guys behind *The Lord of the Rings* and *James Bond*, the project garnered little attention. Somebody in the local paper wrote a column entitled, "Local Kid *Splices* Up His Summer!" I ignored the cheesiness of the headline and focused on the fact that the column was, well, focused on me. For the first time, I felt like I existed in a way that transcended my family and friends.

I was on the planet.

Chapter 2

# HOW TO BEST EXPLODE

*You remember movies but you don't remember your life?*

Adele, *The Majestic*

Mostly suburban, Orange County is more populous than twenty-one states. It's famous for beaches (like Huntington Beach, aka Surf City USA), money (Fortune 500 companies with ambiguous and possibly weapons-manufacturing names like Broadcom and Epicor), and Richard Nixon's house.

There was also a TV show made about our community, which featured lots of thirty-year-olds playing high school students.

In some ways, the OC is heaven on earth. There are no dead-end jobs, and your folks continue to do your laundry indefinitely. We have the largest mall in California and the third largest in the country. In Orange County, it's hard to feel like you need anything in life. Everything is ready-made, even the houses. Rows and rows of cookie-cutter tract homes create the least cinematic environment possible, which explains why we always ended up in the canyon or at least in the custom home sector down the road.

In reality, it is America's retirement community for twentysomethings, and it's where I grew up.

□

My mom was born Tomi (pronounced "Toe-me") Tanabe, which made R-rated video rentals easy for me as a kid.

"Can I get the last name on the account?" the Blockbuster cashier would ask.

"That's Ivie, I-V-I-E."

"Okay. *Tommy*, is that right?"

"Yes, *Tommy Ivie*. And that's *Evil Dead II*, not *III*, right?"

My mom is a Japanese lady, which means she stays very thin, and a woman, which means she thinks her arms are huge in photos. During WWII, the government shipped my mom's mother, uncle, and grandma to an internment camp in Rohwer, Arkansas, after a short stay at the Santa Anita horse stables. Her parents, Marian and Tetsuro Tanabe, were married at the Little White Wedding Chapel in downtown Las Vegas and started their family in the quaint ethnic borough of Montebello, California. Grandpa Tetsuro sadly died before I was old enough to know him. Popular and pretty, Mom represented Montebello in the California Junior Miss Pageant and led the cheer squad, while my uncle Keith set interception records on the football field. My dad says her smile is what made him turn around at a work convention in 1987. I can understand that, and I'm glad that he did.

When I was born, my parents lived in Pasadena in a cute little bungalow with a nice sitting porch. My Grandma T (T for Tanabe) called it a "depression house" because the kitchen drawers were made from old orange crates. My room, she tells me, was the size of a closet, the kind of room where you could reach out and touch opposite walls at the same time. Sometimes I wish I could remember living like that with my parents. Before we had it all.

When I was only a few months old, my parents took a leap of faith and moved us to Mountain Lakes, New Jersey, for my dad's new job. Mountain Lakes is one of those places where characters from John Grisham books go on the lamb. It's serene, cold, and hard to find. We lived in a modest home, with a backyard as big as King Arthur's forest, a forest made for adventurous lads like me. But since the whole house was surrounded by poison ivy, I had to ride my trike on the deck.

Two and a half years later, we were back where the oranges grow, and we never moved again. From my birth forward, my mom became a full-time volunteer. She was a room mom for school and a team mom for T-ball, baseball, basketball, football, soccer, and hockey. Mom was also my emergency contact on every release I ever signed. To this day, she insists that quitting her job and staying home with me were the two best things that ever could have happened.

Personality-wise, my mom is basically a cross between Edna Mode from *The Incredibles* and Mother Teresa. She loves sour candy, *Andy Griffith*, Rick Warren books, and watches only six movies:

- *Marty*
- *Hoosiers*
- *Rudy*
- *The Way We Were*
- *The Sting*
- *All the President's Men* (Rather impressive list if you ask me)

She also secretly plays the piano like the daughter of a Chinese Tiger Mother.

☐

My dad, William Carey Ivie, was born into an Irish Catholic family in Marin County, California. Many years before, his dad— David—served in South Korea as a doctor, where he would set up twelve-bed Quonset hospitals and write letters home to his sweetheart, Patricia.

As a student at Sacred Heart Catholic School, my dad enjoyed playing a game called "Pile on Gregor," in which someone in the schoolyard would yell out, "Pile on Gregor!" and automatically every student in the yard would "pile on" a poor child named Mike Gregor. Dad was the kind of kid who actually lived out all those moments in my favorite movies: pickup baseball games at the local sandlot, chicken fights at recess, and donkey basketball to raise money for poor people.

In the wintertime, he and his scrapper pals made a bad habit of sneaking into the farmer's orchard to pick off walnuts and grapes and dare each other deeper into the brush. The big idea was to see who was the bravest one of the bunch, especially in the midst of patrolling Doberman Pinschers the farmer had let loose into the orchard to protect his assets. Scarier still, of course, was that if the farmer saw you sneaking in, he would immediately mount a large tractor and start rifling rock salt at the slowest intruders.

Good thing my dad was the fastest kid in town.

At home, my dad enjoyed the company of three siblings and was the baby of the family.

When they moved around, my grandma would always label the moving boxes:

- Jack
- Jim
- Sara
- Bill & Misc.

Since I can remember, my dad has been in medical sales and has always been a great provider. In the closet behind his work desk, he still keeps a box of old baseball cards from the days when he had to work the almond ranches to pay for stuff like that. Throughout his life, my dad has always paid his own way, whether it was by way of selling ceiling fans or wood-burning stoves, or crawling underneath houses to hook up the copper line to run water to the fridge.

He was the one who taught me about cars, James Bond (Sean Connery or die), and how to play catch, but our conversations never used to veer much from those topics. I always got the sense that if he could do it all over again, he'd be a bat boy for the 1972 Los Angeles Dodgers and just work his way to GM.

When I was a kid, my dad took me to my first live concert. It was called Aerofest and featured a lot of contemporary Top 40 bands like Styx, REO Speedwagon, and Boston. Looking back, I remember three things from that concert: a large drunk woman sitting in front of us, everyone leaving because Boston waited way too long to play "More Than a Feeling," and my dad fist-pumping and smiling at me to make sure I didn't feel excluded or scared of what drunkenness looked like.

After that night, I listened exclusively to classic rock music for the next three years and even bought a guitar with a scorpion on it.

□

As Steve Martin would say, my brother, Kevin Ivie, "was born a poor black child."[1]

Just kidding.

But he was born really fat, kind of like a baby sumo wrestler. He's since thinned out, but I like to remind him of how far he's come in that area. Kevin is three years younger than me. He and I grew up bunking together until I decided I needed my own space.

As a young pup, he was also very accident prone. In the school-yard, Kevin once crashed his head into a chain-link fence and was immediately rushed to the hospital, where they had to literally staple his head back together. Not long after, he collided with the corner of a wall in our house and became very well known at the San Clemente emergency room. Kevin also got lost often. After a string of very publicized kidnappings in the San Diego area, Kevin disappeared inside a San Diego Nordstrom. Frantic and screaming, Mom marshaled security to shut down the area and bar the doors. No one was allowed in or out. Minutes later, they found little Kevin snickering inside a designer clothing rack in the very center of the emporium. He thought it was hilarious. No one else did.

When Kevin was in elementary school, he first experienced emotional bullying. He acted out a lot in middle school, and our relationship dwindled when we went to separate schools. He went to private school and I went to public.

Like every movie about Catholic school, Kevin and his merry prankster pals terrorized the teachers who weren't cool. Kevin was the kind of kid who swung on flagpoles, mouthed off to the supervisors, and called the flamboyant kids "gay" before they even understood their own feelings. In my imagination, he was being raised by nuns (not really, the school wasn't that old), so I didn't blame him for acting out. His favorite middle school teacher, Mr. Bresert, was like a modern-day Mr. Keating from *Dead Poets Society*. He put up with Kevin and protected him in a way that I didn't.

When my brother and I reconnected in high school, I was usually off excelling and changing the world and he was playing Yu-Gi-Oh at lunch. Apathy became a strong character trait for Kevin because I didn't have that trait. That made him different from me.

Most people knew him as "Brian Ivie's brother."

When Kevin turned eighteen, he stopped going to church. "I am an adult, and I can make my own decisions," he informed my dad one sad morning. Seeing this happen, I made sure to carry on the family tradition.

During the high school years, I didn't say "I love you" much to my parents. At least, not in the way that caught anybody off guard. During dinners, I remember reading labels on condiment bottles and going to bed angry. In the morning, of course, everything was forgiven, or at least filed away somewhere for later. I guess you could say we were very normal. At the same time, I had the feeling even then that there was another way to live. Another way to be a family. I pined for nights when the whole gang would play charades or put on a talent show. I wanted family dinners where people told great stories.

The kind of stories that made my food grow cold.

□

As I began to make more original films and think seriously about being the kind of person who *makes* movies, rather than the kind of person who just *watches* movies, I also began encountering the inevitable pushback from people who were confused or dreadfully concerned.

My parents, who are obviously financially solvent OC suburbanites, even had a growing terror related to my film obsession. I think their arc progressed from "It's a phase," to "Oh no, he's serious," to "I couldn't help but notice how much you like films … maybe you should become an entertainment lawyer!" Very few parents want to see their children strapped into the roller coaster that is making a living in the arts.

But there was a conflict, even in them. As nervous as they were about a film career for me, they were proud of what I was doing. I noticed their smiles and how they would inflate a little when I would string up lights and hang a makeshift screen in the front yard for a film premiere. Maybe I was, in some small way, living the dreams they had allowed to die.

The real blow to my aspirations came when a guy pulled me aside after the article about *Sierra Street* had been written. "It's cool that you had your fifteen minutes of fame," he said. "But you know you're not actually smart and you just copy other peoples' stuff, right?"

I was heartbroken. Who says that to a fifteen-year-old kid?

Usually a sixteen-year-old kid.

I stopped making movies after that for a long time.

☐

I was a Pharisee of film.

Or at least, that's what I became after a lot of comments like the one I got that summer. I didn't wrangle the neighborhood kids together anymore after my freshman year. I just watched movies by myself during lunch, while the guys finally started watching girls during soccer practice.

The movie theater was my church and I was its most devout congregant. It was dark. It was sensory. It was larger than life. There were people there to help me worship (ushers, ticket takers), and I could always count on new films to explore that would feed my growing theology at the time (be special, don't be ordinary, become famous). This guy named G. K. Chesterton once said that "every man who knocks on the door of a brothel is actually searching for God." I guess I was grasping for God too, but I was doing it at suburban Cineplexes and Blockbuster (rest its soul) video stores.

If film was my church, then my operative god was "The Dream." When I watched a movie, I wasn't just watching it—I was imagining myself in it, imagining myself directing it, and imagining myself receiving the accolades for it. I imagined my name in the end credit crawl, and I pictured thousands of people escaping their humdrum lives into the better world I had fashioned for them.

Every day I would watch a movie, and on Friday I'd head to Blockbuster, where the sights (artsy guy behind desk), sounds (a movie playing on overhead televisions), and smells (video cases mixed with candy) were like a second home for me. I'd grab three films for the weekend and sometimes watch all of them on Friday night, finding myself back in the video aisles the next morning. While I was watching, I would never check my phone. Ever. And if someone was going to join me in the dark, they had to abide by the same laws. I had a reverence for, almost a religious fear of, film.

It was a divine thing for me. I believed in Dreams, and I believed that, through film, I would transcend. And besides, I grew up in America, where everybody lives their dreams.

□

In eighth grade, when I was doing Wikipedia searches on 1950s culture to develop my magnum opus, *Sierra Street*, I learned that parents of that time period had lived through the Great Depression. Millions upon millions of Americans were booted from jobs, banks closed like restaurants, and a lot of kids died. After that, people basically decided life was about what you owned. And can you blame them? In the Great Depression, I bet even bacon and eggs seemed like a pat hand.

But in high school, I read a book called *On the Road* by Jack Kerouac.

For anybody who doesn't know, *On the Road,* published in 1957, is basically a three-hundred-page run-on sentence about a group of beatnik friends living out an authentic modern American dream of sex, drugs, and jazz. But for people at that time, and for me in mine, this book said everything I ever wanted to say to Orange County, or to any consumer society.

While reading, I found myself dog-earing pages for the first time and circling paragraphs of truth. "I knew it! I just knew it!" I would say after every chapter. That's how Jack and I became fast friends.

Both of us knew life was more than what you owned.

Jack wrote,

> I realized these were all the snapshots which our children would look at someday with wonder, thinking their parents had lived smooth, well-ordered, stabilized-within-the-photo lives and got up in the morning to walk proudly on the sidewalks of life, never dreaming the raggedy madness and riot of our actual lives, or actual night, the hell of it, the senseless nightmare road. All of it inside endless and beginningless emptiness.[2]

Upstairs in my bedroom, checkered with black-and-white photos of legendary filmmakers, musicians, and entertainers, I found myself comparing the apathetic state of Orange County to that of 1950s America. By this time, I'd read books like *To Kill a Mockingbird,*

*Fahrenheit 451, The Outsiders,* and even *A Separate Peace,* but no one could hold a candle to what I was reading. I wanted more. I knew it was out there, maybe somewhere on the road.

Jack went on,

> The only people for me are the mad ones, the ones who are mad to live, mad to talk, mad to be saved, desirous of everything at the same time, the ones who never yawn or say a commonplace thing, but burn, burn, burn like fabulous yellow roman candles exploding like spiders across the stars and in the middle you see the blue centerlight pop and everybody goes "Awww!"[3]

At the time, my mom's favorite show was *I Love Lucy,* one of the most popular programs of the 1950s. She watched it at night on the TV downstairs. When I came down to grab water, she would tilt her head back on the couch and invite me to have a Popsicle or some other snack and watch with her.

But I never did.

I was too busy planning my escape. Planning my rebellion.

Planning how to best explode.

Chapter 3

# YOU'RE ALREADY DEAD

*I see dead people ... walking around like regular*
*people. They don't know they're dead.*

Cole, *The Sixth Sense*

When I first entered high school, I felt like nobody, not even my own family, took me seriously as an aspiring artist. Out of that, I adopted a posture of "I'm gonna show everybody," which is exhilarating and breathless and raw, but only when things are working out. When you make mistakes you feel rotten, like you just forgot your lines in the Christmas pageant.

In a lot of ways, I was the Jason Schwartzman character in any Wes Anderson movie. You know the Max Fischer character in the prep school movie *Rushmore*? The kid who stages his own shows, makes up his own clubs (Rushmore Beekeepers Society), goes out for the wrestling team (he's an alternate), and tries to get Mr. Blume to fund a giant aquarium, all so he can impress the Olivia Williams character? That was me, save the student-teacher-millionaire love triangle thing. I thought that living my dream, and staving off the ordinary life, would somehow redeem me.

"I'll show them," I bellowed like a mad genius. "I'll show them all."

Scene 1: I'm forced by my soccer coach to stand
in front of the metal lockers, on one of those little

narrow benches, and tell my teammates why I'm quitting the team, which is to go (that day) to a dance audition for a role in our school's production of *Footloose*. In the John Hughes (*Breakfast Club, Sixteen Candles, Ferris Bueller*, etc.) movie version, it would have been the football team, and my coach would have been pro–gun rights and florid, with a crew cut. In my version, the coach is weirdly supportive, and the British assistant coach who just loves soccer smiles and tears up like I'm leaving for the Western Front.

Ultimately, I get the only nondancing role in *Footloose*. Go figure.

It's relevant to know that I went out for soccer in the first place because I was terrified of gym class and wanted to get out of having to take it—an admission that fits perfectly with the John Hughes ethos of what I wrote above.

Scene 2: I am a published film critic as a teenager and start my own boutique film production company. I also build my out-of-print and Criterion DVD collections and have a cinema club (I *am* Max Fischer from *Rushmore*) at which a small group of film nerds discusses movies like *Glengarry Glen Ross* and makes short film noirs.

My lack of success with women is a surprise to no one at this point.

Scene 3: I cry in my mom and dad's bedroom because I have no friends, have no girlfriend, and am terrified of speaking in public, although I desperately want to be president of my high school.

Scene 4: I become the lead singer and rhythm guitar player for an Orange County garage band called Arts and Crafts. Pause for a moment to appreciate how truly horrible that name is. We are sort of an early Clapton meets Linkin Park meets the *Juno* soundtrack sorta thing. Inexplicably, during shows I wear a black bandana and sing with a noticeable British accent. However, even more inexplicably, girls really like it, and I get my first hits of both female admiration and marijuana.

Scene 5: I am kicked out of Arts and Crafts for dancing with the bass player's crush and then proceeding to kiss the bass player's crush. The band claims they are simply "going in a new direction." Tragically, Orange County loses a great garage band and has to find someone else to play "Hey Jude" and "Free Fallin'" at house parties.

Scene 6: I am finally voted student body president my senior year. On a white board in a classroom, somebody writes, "Brian Ivie rules." I also get into USC, the Harvard of film schools.

I came. I saw. I conquered.

In a town like San Clemente, there's only one local theater, so for most big film premieres, I ended up seeing hundreds of classmates there. Despite flagrant phone use, it tended to be fun with friends. One of my favorite memories was going to see *Pirates of the Caribbean: At World's End*. To clarify, I went with about half the class, flirted with a girl, and didn't watch much of the movie. But I'll always remember one character: Bootstrap Bill Turner.

It didn't escape me at the time that he shared the name Bill with my dad.

In the scene I'll always remember, Elizabeth Swan (Keira Knightley) searches the depths of The Flying Dutchman dungeons for a man named Bootstrap Bill, the father of Orlando Bloom's character, Will Turner.

Calling out his name into the cells, Elizabeth finds Bill literally lodged into the wall of the ship, with coral growing all over his body.

"Tell him to stay away. Tell him it's too late. I'm already part of the ship," says Bootstrap after hearing that his son is supposedly coming to the rescue. It's actually a genuinely sad moment in an overwhelmingly superficial film. Elizabeth can't do anything but watch him sink back into the wooden walls from whence he came.

From that day forward, I couldn't get Bootstrap Bill's coral-covered grimace out of my head. To me, anyone who didn't fulfill their dream or destiny just faded away like the man in that movie. They became part of the ship, part of a creaking and crumbling existence. And I had made a vow long ago that I would never let that happen to me.

Growing up, I had (and probably still have) a really serious fear of an ordinary life. I was Haley Joel Osment, and I saw dead people everywhere I looked. Shuffling into cubicles, driving their midsized sedans, and socking money away into their 401ks. When you don't do what you're made to do, you're already dead. That was my motto.

"I don't want to live in a world without love or grief or beauty. I'd rather die," says Becky in *Invasion of the Body Snatchers*. Now, that was a woman who understood life.

I didn't want a regular career and I didn't want a regular love life either. I feared becoming the jaundiced dad who coached his kids in roller hockey but stopped holding his wife's hand. I always wanted to say "I love you" to someone and have her say it back. I just wanted to yell it, like Clark Gable did in *It Happened One Night*. I was a hopeless romantic—the kind of guy who would go sit on a cliff and look at the ocean and dream about someone who could put sunscreen on my back. I felt like I had a lot of love to offer, almost like I'd stored it up from hardly ever sharing love with my own family.

As a result, I fell in and out of "love" all the time. I was relentlessly sentimental. I wanted the excitement and the little "shot of love" (Bob Dylan) that comes from a new message in my inbox or another suggestive text. I wanted the flirty look across the room at a party. I wanted first kisses. Lots of them. From lots of people.

Then a girl with big blue eyes came on the scene. She was sixteen. I was barely seventeen. Her grandfather was a minister, she had never had a boyfriend before, and she liked me.

I was at a friend's house, and I saw her from across the room, dressed in a soft violet like someone out of the 1950s. She smiled at me. It was the kind of smile you feel is reserved for you, and I had never seen her before. It felt like one of those star-crossed moments.

So in perfect form, I started dating a different girl a few weeks later.

After that plane crashed, I looked up the mystery girl with the blue eyes, and we really hit it off. Poetry in motion. She knew all the other girls I'd made out with and was willing to work with it. I really don't want to be trivial, because she really did change my ways. And for a few years I devoted myself to her, hopelessly and romantically, and we loved to say, "I love you."

Before we started going steady, my romantic bible was a book called *The Great Gatsby*. Most people know this book as the story of a mysterious millionaire named Jay Gatsby, who falls for a beautiful dame named Daisy. In other words, the common understanding of this book is that Jay loves Daisy, obsessively maybe, but he still truly loves her.

The way I read it now is as a story of a man who *loves himself and wants to be the author of his own life*. And in the life story of Jay Gatsby, written by Jay Gatsby, Daisy Buchanan has faithfully loved him and only him her whole life. That's why when Daisy admits to having once loved another man named Tom toward the end of the book, Gatsby furiously refuses to accept it. He won't accept a love from her that isn't the one he wrote. It has to be his way, his story, his script.

In the end, the tragedy of Fitzgerald's book isn't that Gatsby can't win Daisy's heart. It's that he doesn't really want Daisy at all. He wants only the caricature of her that he's dreamed up in his head.

Of course, this isn't selfless love; it's self-love. Which is really no love at all.

Once, I remember, I threw my keys in the gutter outside my girlfriend's house because she was "acting weird." She wasn't acting the way I wanted in response to my love. I had these mental scripts written for our relationship, but she kept saying the wrong lines. But I had told myself I would never yell at a woman, let alone a girl.

So much for that. I screamed at her.

Like Gatsby, I loved my girlfriend only according to how I wanted her to be.

Over time, my heart wandered through the desert for other outlets, for other things to fill me up inside. I had availed myself to romance and it just didn't complete me like the movies said it would. Sorry I'm not sorry, Jerry Maguire.

When I exhausted the film dream (for a time), I turned to a girl. When I exhausted the girl, I turned back to film. When I exhausted film again, I turned to porn.

I still remember that first time I saw a picture I wasn't supposed to see. It was a Britney Spears sticker from one of those nickel-nickel arcade machines. For a sheltered OC kid, Britney Spears, dripping in green mesh and frozen midsong, was nothing short of revelatory. At this point, the closest relationship I had to a visual like this, mind you, was the scene of singing sirens in my *Odyssey* summer reading for school. Of course, this was before laptops and Internet searches made the whole world "nickel-nickel." But from that point on, I was always looking for better, faster ways of looking at stuff I wasn't supposed to.

Problem was, no one ever actually told me I wasn't supposed to. Not even my longtime girlfriend. So I dated her into college and slept with my computer on the side.

Not unlike the actual beatniks and hippies who came before me, my desire for transcendence led me to just as much emptiness as it did real emotion. Sex, drugs, and rock 'n' roll sound great when the only alternative is no sex, television, and a long retirement. But maybe that wasn't the only option out there. It took longer to reach the shores of disillusion, but my rebellious worldview was starting to wear as thin as the veil hanging over picture-perfect Orange County.

Why didn't I feel alive?

Enter Will Tober, the buffest Evangelical Christian in three counties.

Chapter 4

---

# GOD'S WILL

*Truman Burbank: Was nothing real?*
*Christof: You were real. That's what made you so good to watch ...*
*The Truman Show*

Growing up in America, I always figured I was a Christian. I didn't smoke cigarettes, I went to Mass with my dad, and I watched Fox News with my mom. I prayed the rosary off and on and tried to do the right thing. But my faith was a personal place, played close to the chest. Evangelicals, on the other hand, were a totally different species.

They were the ones in movies who ignorantly condemned all the authentic main characters (think Amanda Bynes in *Easy A*). They were the ones on the news blasting gays or screaming at fourteen-year-old girls carrying the children of a date rape. Evangelical Christians were suckers, busybodies, hypocrites, haters, or just people who needed a crutch because something really bad had happened. I didn't blame that last group. I believed in God. I believed everything happened for a reason. I'm pretty sure John Locke from *Lost* made that very clear. But I didn't believe everyone else had to believe in order to escape hell. That sounded like the most ignorant crap I'd ever heard.

Everybody had his own way of believing, and religion for me was way more about this life than the next. Religion was about empowering me to live this life to the fullest, to my happiest. I didn't think about religion as a way to transcend eternal death. If religion was good for anything, it was good for empowering my life here and now.

Right now.

Scene 1: We find ourselves in San Clemente High School's gymnasium. It's nighttime. A throng of glow-in-the-dark high schoolkids in a wide range of pop-culture costumes has gathered around a big stage for an Air Guitar Battle, which is yet another opportunity to be impressed by the best-looking, most-popular kids in school. Enter Will Tober—dressed in white spandex and a wifebeater. If this was an eighties movie about a high school in California, Will's part would be played by Rob Lowe or Corey Haim. Anyway, Will gets funky to an 'N Sync song, and, as you can imagine, the girls go crazy because Will is just about the most beefcakey guy I've ever met. Broad shoulders. Lantern jaw (as they say). And a terrific dancer.

Will's favorite move was the one where you bend down, slap the floor, and "do the worm" all the way back up. Yes, I know, absolutely disgusting.

Will was a fascinating guy because he was a Christian who didn't seem to be hiding everything. In addition to the perfect features, dancing skills, and well-to-do OC family pedigree, Will also happened to be the star of the football team. He's the kind of kid you want to hate, just out of principle.

But Will was genuine and we shared a dream of going to USC.

In our junior year of high school, I decided I needed to put Will's physical attributes to work in my film *Shelter*. In my first horror film, a kid goes missing and his brother has to find him, which, of course, involves going down into the sewer system. Because who doesn't want to shoot a low-budget high school film in the city sewer system? I cast Will as kind of an arrogant jerk character. In addition to being phenomenally bad as an actor, he just couldn't be a jerk.

But there's nothing like shooting a film in the sewer to bond people. We jumped the fence, and we did it together. We bonded to the degree that even though we were very different, we roomed together at USC our freshman year and bunked in the biggest party dorm on campus. Upon first meeting our next-door neighbors, I sarcastically suspected they were drug dealers. Later that semester, our neighbors were arrested because they were actually major campus-wide drug dealers.

Back in high school, Will seemed to look up to me, which is weird to think about now. But according to several tiny local newspapers, I was going places, and I told him to hang on if he wanted to come.

At USC, Will and I would lie in our beds at night, look up at the ceiling, and talk about God. I developed an arsenal of impossible theological questions, from "Did Adam have a belly button?" all the way to "What about the guy on the deserted island without a Bible? Does he go to hell just because he couldn't find a way home like Tom Hanks did in *Cast Away?*"

Will would listen patiently and, most of the time, just honestly say, "I don't know."

He stumbled through the gospel message with me on a few occasions, but more than anything, he kept inviting me to these corny "worship nights" in the quad, where mediocre musicians would play unplugged Christian alt music and everyone would hold hands. Even though I wasn't yet a member of this apparent cult, Will was honest with me about his growth pattern as a Christian. It was very volatile, and he never hid or buried anything. In that, he was a model for authenticity. We got along great. Then one day ...

Scene 2:

"Hey, Will?" I say.

"I don't know," he instinctively retorts.

"I haven't even asked you anything yet," I continue.

"Okay, shoot, Bri."

"What does truth mean to you?"

"Well, I guess it means that some things are false."

"Do you think everyone but Christians are false?" I provoke.

"I wouldn't say it exactly like that, but yeah."

"That just doesn't seem right to me."

"Why?"

"Everybody has their own truth, I feel like. Their own individual truth. It doesn't matter really; it's just for them."

A beat.

"I wholeheartedly disagree with that."

Will's answer went with me the rest of the semester. I pushed a lot of buttons, but that was the first time he'd actually said anything stern.

After that, Will started inviting me to these Campus Crusade (also known as CRU) meetings. Ironically, they were a lot like going to a movie. Big crowd, dark room. You could be as interpersonally engaged or aloof as you wanted to be. And even though they were

pretty slickly packaged with the music and the lighting and everything, it wasn't lame. And they didn't seem like they were necessarily
trying to sell anything.

I wanted to run, but I couldn't, because going to those meetings was sort of like watching a Spielberg film about aliens. You
know you're going to alien places, but for some reason you feel safe
with Spielberg, like he's going to guide you through it in one piece,
no matter how many things explode along the way. That's how I
felt at CRU.

When I was in film school, I always wore a leather jacket and a
ball cap because that's how I thought directors dressed. I wanted
to be Christopher Nolan. We all did. In the beginning, everybody in film school wants to be a director and everybody talks
about how much they love *Pulp Fiction* or, if they're really cool,
*Reservoir Dogs*. But as the years go by most people get funneled
into post-production and end up admitting how they actually
love *Remember the Titans*.

Films, historically, have been a huge part of our culture, which
is a big part of the draw for me. In the early years of the industry,
films were transportive and cheap, and they gave people an escape.
They also offered a sense of belonging, imagination, enculturation.
In college, films taught me how to be a person of the world, how to
talk, how to kiss, how to live.

Early in my time at USC, I even wrote this on a class syllabus:

I feel like I was born to make movies. I know that sounds trite, but it's not something I can simply stop doing. It's a compulsion, but in the most positive sense. I have an incredible passion for the art form and if I wasn't doing it, it would be like I wasn't truly living.

On one end, I had Will telling me how to live (in a relationship with God), and on the other I had film professors saying things like, "The world is in trouble. The world is bleeding. Cinema is a messiah machine that can recover us and return us to a sense that the world is meaningful, instead of the slaughterhouse we turn it into."

I wasn't like Will then, but I was still grappling with issues of truth. I wondered if, in the quiet moments, my teachers really believed what they were selling: the idea that if "photography is truth," then in film, truth happens twenty-four frames a second. It's the kind of thing that's supposed to instill you with a sense of nobility in your craft.

As a freshman, I scribbled those notes into my notebook, feeling like I was really on the ground floor of the meaning of life.

Obviously, it's easy to feel that way about a movie like *Chariots of Fire* or *Dead Poets Society* but much harder to feel that way about *White Chicks*. Still, phrases like that were like auditory cocaine for a bunch of cocky but secretly insecure hipsters whose short films got rejected from midlevel film festivals across the nation. Maybe we needed to feel like we were saving the world, one movie at a time.

Or maybe we needed to feel like making movies was going to save us.

□

When I would come back from class, I remember, Will would be scrubbing through schmaltzy online videos about mission trips he could take with CRU. But strangely, he always stayed home during the summer and made films with me. For both of us, I think, films were analogous to our relationships with women—it was all about being a part of something bigger than yourself, something potentially epic. That was the draw of film, and that was the draw of serially dating different girls.

The summer after our freshman year, we made a feature-length narrative film called *Farmer's Tan*. It was a movie about high school, friendship, and all of my emotional problems. We held actual auditions (even though we still cast mostly friends) and shot the film over the span of three weeks with the latest and greatest DSLR cameras.

One night, Collin (the kid who got hit with the devil's fork earlier) showed up looking sad. We were working really late that night—I'm talking till three in the morning—so I couldn't have any discouraging attitudes on set.

Collin's mom had died the day before.

I offered meager condolences and told Collin he could leave, but secretly wanted him to stay. I had worked way too hard and Collin was the bass in our barbershop quartet. We needed four voices.

As one would expect, it was nearly impossible for him to smile or stay on pitch, so I kept cutting the scene to fix him. We all knew his mom was going to die, it wasn't a surprise, and he showed up to the set, which said to me that he was just fine. By hook or by crook we got through, and around 4:00 a.m. I congratulated the team for working extra hard to realize my vision. I hugged all the stage parents for staying late with their kids and hurriedly thanked Collin for soldiering through.

Since I had moved to San Clemente, Collin and his family had lived right down the road from me. He was an old friend who always played Gimli when we made *Fellowship*. I also knew his mom at her best, before anything bad happened. But when I was in director mode, people weren't people to me.

They were plot devices. Not just in *Farmer's Tan* but in my amazing, authentic, beautiful, real life.

Chapter 5

# JUNE 20, 2011

*Someone has to die in order that the rest of us should value life more.*

Virginia, *The Hours*

I was eating pancakes on the morning of June 20, 2011, reading the *Los Angeles Times*. It was a typical Orange County morning, perfectly sunny and eighty degrees. Out the window of our breakfast nook, past the hot tub and beyond the rolling hills, lay my charmed life. As the Ron Livingston character says in *Swingers*, it was "manifest destiny."

At the very bottom of the front page was a weird photo of a man holding a baby inside this small hatch. There was a pull-out quote too, containing the words shown on a sign on the box itself: "This is a facility for the protection of life. If you can't take care of your disabled babies, don't throw them away or leave them on the street. Bring them here."

Bring them here. Bring them here. I turned that phrase over in my mind like the pancakes my mom was turning over on the stove.

Riveted, I cracked open the paper and my eyes began to dance like mad, flicking up and down and left to right without skipping a word. I read the paper like I used to read *On The Road*. Like a starving man. It was a story that I thought shouldn't exist. That's what made it so great. A story about a pastor who had built a depository for disabled babies.

"'In the mid-1980s,' Lee said, 'the disabled in South Korea were often viewed as embarrassing curiosities—more creature than child.'"

In South Korea today, it went on to explain, cosmetic surgeries are "as common as haircuts" and disabilities are still viewed as "national shame."

Then there was the part about the pastor's own son.

"The baby was born with cerebral palsy. A mammoth cyst on his head choked off the blood flow, slowly rendering him brain-damaged. Doctors gave him months to live. Today he lies on a bed in Lee's home, his legs splayed at impossible angles, his feet turned back inward.... He occasionally lets out a snort or sigh, as his parents regularly vacuum his saliva through a tracheal hole.... I asked God, 'Why would you give me a handicapped child?' I wasn't grateful for this baby,' Lee recalled."

*Where's the photo? Where's the boy?* My mind churned. I looked around for scissors to cut the article loose from the surrounding articles on golf. For the first time in my life, the front page of the *LA Times* somehow applied to me.

"Strangely," the *Times* writer continued, "the boy Lee once blamed on God ended up bringing him closer to his faith."

I read the article five more times and didn't dare skim.

"The drop box is attached to the side of a home in a ragged working-class neighborhood. It is lined with a soft pink and blue blanket, and has a bell that rings when the little door is opened. Because this depository isn't for books, it's for babies—and not just any infants; these children are the unwanted ones, a burden many parents find too terrible to bear. One is deaf, blind and paralyzed; another has a tiny misshapen head. There's a baby with Down syndrome, another with cerebral palsy, still another who is quadriplegic, with permanent brain damage.

"But to Pastor Jong-rak Lee, they are all perfect. And they have found a home here at the ad hoc orphanage he runs with his wife and small staff."[4]

I'd studied love. I'd read Keats and Housman. I'd seen *Casablanca* and *Gone with the Wind*. But I'd never seen love like Pastor Lee's love for these broken, forgotten children. It was a love that, honestly, looked a lot dirtier and a lot less fun than I thought it should.

I wondered about this as my pancakes shriveled up on the edges. Then, looking at the plate before me, a thought exploded in my brain like one of Jack Kerouac's roman candles across the sky:

A story just made my food grow cold.

□

Angry, bewildered, and inspired, I immediately fired off an email to the reporter from the *Times*, assuming that thousands of other desperate student filmmakers, if not Ken Burns himself, were right then simultaneously plotting to make this man's story into the next Sundance Grand Jury Prize documentary.

I remember writing something like this:

*Dear LA Times,*

*Greetings. My name is Brian Ivie, the director of Sierra [backspace, backspace, backspace, backspace, backspace, backspace] of many short films and features. I am a rising junior at the University of Southern California's School of Cinematic Arts and would like to connect with*

*Pastor Jong-rak Lee of Ju-sarang Community Church about a potential documentary film endeavor. I can be reached through my assistant at info@flashbulbentertainment.com. Thank you and keep on dreaming.*

*Brian Ivie*
*President and CEO*
*Flashbulb Entertainment, LLC*
*[company was real, assistant was not]*

Literally less than a minute later I received a reply from a correspondent in South Korea named JY Choi, who provided all relevant contact information. Like a one-two punch, I lit off an impassioned email to the pastor himself … aaaaaaaand it bounced back to me.

I sent another email, and it bounced back to me. I sent emails like people push crosswalk buttons. In the end, I probably tried twelve times before resolving to pour a quart of syrup over my old flapjacks.

I'd never been out of the country at that point besides a cruise to Mexico and a short trip to Canada, neither of which really count. At the time, I was still essentially making movies in a way that felt safe to me. I wasn't in the back canyon anymore, but I was still making stuff about me. I was making movies that said what I believed, what I wanted to say. "Maybe it's a good thing this pastor never got my email," I murmured. "Maybe it's God's way of saying, 'You don't just email people you see in pictures and then make movies on their lives.'" That sounded like God to me at the time. "This is clearly a sign that I'm not supposed to go to South Korea," I concluded.

And yet, I held out hope for something amazing to happen.

A month later, I was sitting at my girlfriend's place, and my computer let out a soft ding.

I had mail. But I had no idea how that sound, that ding, would come full circle in a few short months. I crawled over to my MacBook and selected my USC mail window, expecting either spam or a film festival rejection notice from someplace like Spartanburg, South Carolina, or Rome (Georgia, not Italy). Instead, I received the following Google-translated message:

*Dear Brian,*

*Hello, nice meet you. I don't know what it means to make documentary film. But you can course come and live with me if you want.*

*Sincerely,*
*Jong-rak Lee*

*Maybe God wanted me to win Sundance after all.*

In the email, Pastor Lee had attached a PowerPoint presentation on what he hoped to accomplish with his ministry, and how he wanted grass outside so the kids could play. I clicked through the PowerPoint, which had jarring images of the children with strange, squished faces and arms that ended at the wrist.

The slides told me he and his staff would take in kids other people couldn't afford, hence all the issues with their faces and limbs and stuff. Some of the kids were abandoned in hospitals; others were left on the doorstep of their creaky old house.

Even with all the clipart and goofy fonts, there was something real about this. It was certainly different from the youth-group-meets-obligation talk I had experienced before. It sounded a lot more like Will did in the dorms, returning my authentic questions with authentic answers.

Based on scattered dates, I surmised that the box for babies was the newest addition to the pastor's orphanage. But it made sense. "The guy must own a restaurant to feed all those abandoned kids," I reasoned.

"Why not build a drive-through?"

□

Right then, my plan was to scrape together whatever crappy cameras we had and make a ten- to twenty-minute short film. In my heart of hearts, I wanted to make the film to help those babies, but I also wanted to help myself become extremely famous.

"If we don't get to Sundance by 2013," I informed my crew very dramatically, "it's over."

Standing in McCarthy quad one night, I told Will and my Asian friend, Bryce Komae, about my latest (first-ever) cross-global filmmaking jaunt. "Guys, I'm going to Korea," I revealed with a grin. Bryce was an Evangelical as well. The hipster kind. We'd need him to make a trendy Christian film about Asian issues.

At first this didn't really register with them, the way study abroad program admittance doesn't register with USC kids who have traveled to several continents before they can drink (except where they study abroad). As on most college campuses, studying abroad was popular at USC, and the Dornsife school pushed it with glossy brochures and pictures of Santorini. This imagery was just a standard part of life for kids our age. And these guys had been around me, cameras, and my crazy ideas for years. Still, I wanted them to be excited about South Korea.

It's important to note, at this point, that I had absolutely no connection to South Korea whatsoever, except my friend Sam Jo, who I originally thought was Chinese. And in fact, I hated to travel. I hated airplanes and recycled oxygen. I liked making movies in my hometown, where things were familiar and where I used to get ambushed with my best friends. Plus, this was before Instagram got big, so we'd have to start a blog page if we wanted people to see us being cultured and awesome.

But pieces started falling into place in surprising ways. For one, there was a Korean guy named Jin Doo, who happened to come to my house for Thanksgiving because he was interning with my uncle. He heard about the project and said, "I'll come and translate. My family lives really close to the pastor."

Boom. Easy.

Shortly thereafter we started the desperate, albeit well-meaning, Kickstarter campaign. For those of you who don't know about

Kickstarter, it's essentially an online fundraising platform where you set a financial goal for a movie, album, or piece of technology you are too poor to produce and proceed to beg your friends and extended family to help you reach it. At the time, Kickstarter wasn't yet in vogue but was just starting to emerge as the quintessential crowd-funding platform for amateur filmmakers. I remember talking with Will as we were setting up the page. "How much do you think we should try to raise? Is five thousand too much to ask for?" I asked.

"Why not raise ten thousand?" Will dared. My smile stretched up my face like the grinch who stole Christmas.

After a short "prayer," I posted an appeal for twenty thousand large.

"Let's see what this God can really do," I mumbled.

After that, it felt like we were just logging in each day and watching the meter tick upward. It was crazy. People I didn't know from all around the world with usernames like Growth Capital Corp and Loveyoulexaloo donated to the cause, and I was forced to start speaking a lot of Christianese. I even got an opportunity to share in front of the Campus Crusade group about the film and definitely found myself putting on Christian airs. That part was easy. I roomed with the buffest Christian in three counties.

"Thanks for your donation! Have a blessed day!"

"Thanks so much! For His glory!"

"Gosh, thank you! Maranatha!"

Different groups asked me for letters of recommendation from a pastor. I didn't have a pastor, so I asked a professor I knew, who was a Catholic priest, to write a letter for me. I in no way felt qualified for what I was undertaking … especially as the dollar amounts continued to rise.

But we raised all the money without breaking a sweat.

To be fair, I questioned myself in private moments, as much as I questioned Pastor Lee. We knew nothing about this man besides what we'd read in a couple of emails and an article. There was a lot of investment riding on very little information. At the same time, I didn't know much about God and relied on Will to keep everything kosher (so to speak). Still, the Kickstarter campaign seemed to inspire people who had dreams and resources but perhaps couldn't go themselves. It struck a chord. Then one day I got a cryptic call from a friend of a friend.

"I'd like to match the twenty thousand dollars you raised on Kickstarter," he said.

"Why?" I replied honestly.

"You'll understand later," he whispered like the grandpa in *National Treasure*.

Parents of another classmate wrote me a twenty-five-thousand-dollar check a few days after that. For those of you playing at home, that's sixty-five thousand dollars for a ten-minute movie. Something bigger than me was clearly afoot.

After the campaign closed another USC student, Sarah Choi, approached me in the quad. She was also Korean, not Chinese as I had first suspected.

"How are you planning on budgeting and scheduling this trip?" she asked.

"Sarah," I retorted, "why don't you be my producer and handle all of those annoying details?"

"I'll be a second translator too. You'll probably need that for certain situations," she said with a smile.

"Amen," I said with a slight oriental bow.

From that day forward, Sarah essentially became my manager. One day, she had me hop on the phone with a friend of her mom. At this point, these calls could mean only one thing:

Thousands of dollars.

The woman didn't have 20K to offer out of the gate, but she had read the article from the *LA Times* and happened to be the wife of the president of Oakley Optics, makers of the state-of-the-art RED Camera. Having already purchased tickets and all other forms of equipment, I asked Laura if she would buy me the newest RED movie camera, the yet-to-be-released RED Scarlet. Her response: "Of course."

A few days later, I walked into the RED showroom in Irvine and walked out with about fifty thousand dollars in equipment. With the extra money, we also rented a RED Epic, mostly because Peter Jackson was shooting *The Hobbit* on the same camera at the same time.

My little project had become something much, much bigger. And for better or worse, it had very little to do with me.

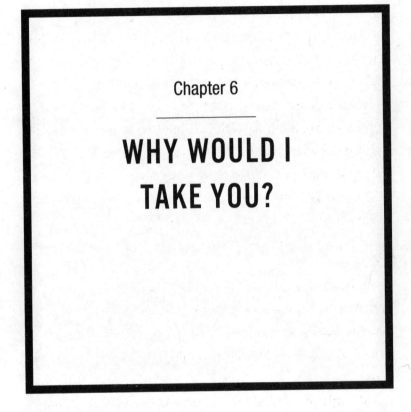

Chapter 6

# WHY WOULD I TAKE YOU?

*Pippin: Anyways, you need people of intelligence*
*on this sort of mission ... quest ... thing.*
*Merry: Well, that rules you out, Pip.*
*The Lord of the Rings: The Fellowship of the Ring*

Now that we had the money, it was time to get the team back together. I crossed oceans to find the perfect technicians. I left no stone unturned. Not unlike my old days, the crew was divided equally between men and women. Nine guys, two girls. When it was all over, we flew eleven of Southern California's finest from LAX to Incheon, all of whom ended up being devastatingly underqualified for every position on a normal film production crew:

## JIN DOO: TRANSLATOR

- My uncle's best intern
- Member of the Korean army for four years
- Claims to have fallen asleep while marching
- Potentially a government spy

## SAM JO: PRODUCER/TRANSLATOR

- Not Chinese
- Business student with no film experience whatsoever

- Hasn't spoken Korean in years
- Definitely a government spy

## SARAH CHOI: PRODUCER/TRANSLATOR

- Personal manager
- Sang in a Christian youth choir (not helpful here)
- Interned at Creative Artist's Agency (CAA)
- Would meet her current boyfriend while making the film

## TAVIS ROBERTSON: KEY GRIP

- Best-looking member of the team (besides Will)
- Mostly an actor
- No history as a key grip
- Nominal Christian

## SHAYAN EBRAHIM: DIRECTOR OF PHOTOGRAPHY

- Raised in Iran
- Son of my dentist
- Good with cameras but had never used the ones we rented
- Skinnier than me (finally)

## STERLING PHILLIPS: PHOTOGRAPHER/PA

- Only non-Korean girl
- Film student and documentary buff
- Texas born, where everyone is a Christian
- Would later make a documentary on rave culture

## BRYCE KOMAE: COMPOSER

- Sexy singer-songwriter
- Half-Japanese (Together, we make one full Asian)
- Hipster Christian
- While in South Korea, used Spanish to communicate with a store owner

## MITCH MCDUFF: DIRECTOR OF PHOTOGRAPHY (PART 2)

- Recreational playwright
- Went to film school online (Watched random YouTube videos)
- Once built a boat for fun
- In high school

## WILL TOBER: PRODUCER

- Team chaplain
- Jacked

- Famous for coining the term "Korea toes" to describe the cold
- Jacked

## KEVIN IVIE: SOUND RECORDIST

- My baby brother
- Read the microphone manual on the flight over
- Spent off-hours writing a love letter to a girl back home
- Loved the kids most

With a team in place, I tried to get my mind around how to shoot a documentary. It was something I'd obviously never done before, let alone in another language. I still have a sheet of notebook paper on which my friend Josh Woo scrawled basic phrases out for me like "How much?" or "Where is the bathroom?" Just looking at it made me nervous. For a guy who was used to being an adept, charming, funny, and manipulative communicator, I was about to go to a place where I would be none of those things.

As the days rushed by that fall, I began interviewing Korean USC students about plastic surgery. Going right along with the *LA Times* article, I started to pit the pastor's "deformed flock" against the plastic-surgery-happy culture that I believed he was rebelling against. According to many students, South Korea was the plastic surgery capital of the world. The land of new noses and new faces, where it really did seem "as common as a haircut." This fascinated me, especially as my acne issues gave way to noticeable scars. In the mirror back home, I would often roll my fingers across the pockmarks on my cheeks. Turning my face, I pulled my skin taut until the scars would disappear. As I ridiculed others, I wondered about costs for laser surgery to change how I felt about my profile.

□

Scene 1: I'm sitting with my mom as she cries over my brother's college application essay. The title is "In His Shadow." It's about how I was the lead in the school play and the valedictorian of our high school and how I got accepted to the most elite film school in the world. He was, to be honest, tired of seeing me succeed and tired of seeing me celebrated and tired of being forgotten in all of it.

My mom shows me the essay and we have that weird moment when she is watching me read something and looking for my reaction, and it's clear there's a reaction she wants/expects. She sort of stands there with her hands on her hips as I read and looks at me like, "Well … well?"

To be honest, I didn't have much insight into Kevin's emotions as they were happening because they were happening to *him*, and he was infinitely less interesting because he wasn't *me*. And at some point in our family history, I had stopped knowing him. Or maybe I stopped trying.

We saw each other on vacations.

But I did remember the drawings he did. He drew pictures of us playing together in ways that we never actually did (except in the neighborhood movies)—running around with swords and shields and stuff. I guess he was drawing the things he *wanted* to do with me. When I invited Kevin to help me with the film, it was, he says, one of the most significant moments of his life. We needed someone to hold the boom pole. So it wasn't a tearful reconciliation, but it was a start.

Scene 2: I'm in my room, going through the email attachments the pastor had sent to me upon first contact. I brush through the PowerPoint again and learn that the pastor's home is legally a church that adopts and guards children who have no other options. But not just any kids. It's the seemingly most disposable of the lot. The ones with pieces missing. Based on the PowerPoint, Lee's church provides:

- Cohabitation for the disabled
- Counseling and healing for families with disabled children (basically helping them deal with reality)
- Aid for the disabled, including education
- The "baby box," as an option over abortion and abandonment of the disabled (the box idea still freaks me out a bit)

Reading on, I don't feel informed enough to address abortion. I don't even have an opinion on it, but the slides start showing how disabled kids are often prenatally screened and killed. One of the kids in the slideshow (who by his picture looks like he's got Down syndrome) was removed from his mother's womb at seven months and was not given any water to drink. Now he lives at Lee's place. I wonder then if I'll meet the little boy soon, and I wonder what it will be like to see him drink water from little Dixie cups.

The pictures of their house are dismal. They remind me of where my parents lived before my dad started doing well at work. Cramped, claustrophobic even. An entire slide is dedicated to needing an elevator because some of the kids would need new legs in order to use the stairs. Pastor Lee also mentions a bathtub, ventilation that could keep the whole house from reeking of adult diapers, and lower windows so that even the kids who can't walk up the steep stairs can see what color the sky is.

"To people with disability God could be a cruel person who gives them pain and despair instead of love and blessing. To people who have difficulty accepting Heaven's peace we serve them with Jesus Christ's heart, because there's no other special way to tell them the Gospel," reads one of the slides.[5]

In the moment, I don't know exactly what this means, but given the number of disabled kids they care for, I figure this is probably the most holy place in the universe and decide it's time to buy a cross necklace on Amazon for when I meet the pastor. My mom had given me a dog tag with a Bible verse on it, but after watching *Full Metal Jacket* I just don't feel like an army chain is the right vibe for a Christian director. Plus, the cross seems to be this rallying cry for Christians who donated to our project, so I go for that.

Later on, I figure, I will appear in still photographs and behind-the-scenes video clips wearing the necklace, which people will assume has a really amazing story behind it like, "I whittled it out of wood when I was living with bushmen in Africa," or "I found it near the house I built with Amigos for Christ."

Scene 3: I'm seated in my dad's office, shortly after reading the article and raising the money to go to South Korea. In my parents' minds this has gone from, "Oh, that's nice, Brian" to "Oh ----, this is actually happening." My dad's office is right next to my bedroom. It isn't what you'd expect from the quintessential successful guy's office. No aquarium, no minibar, no resolute desk. Just lots of miniature football helmets, tin soldiers, golf-related knickknacks, and family photos of me and him throughout the years. My dad has freckles and sandy hair, combed over. Blue eyes, not brown. He's seated in his chair, with his arms folded and concern etched all over his kind face.

"Brian, you ... you can't go," he stammers.

I insist that I am, indeed, going. The money is raised and I'm going to South Korea.

"Then I want to go with you. You and your brother are all I have. What if something goes wrong?" he protests.

I know he's taking pressure from his friends, one of whom really railed on him for letting me "study abroad with Kim Jong Il." When you plan trips to South Korea, you find out really fast that Americans

still think there's a war going on there. But it is a watershed moment
for me. A moment in which I have the opportunity to invite my dad
back into my life and help him understand what I do and why I do it.
There was a time when I allowed my dad into my filmmaking
life. He was, after all, the camera operator for *Sierra Street*. I'm not
saying he should stop selling heart valves and walk on at Paramount,
but he held the camera so I didn't have to. He also drove six hours to
his hometown (where we were shooting) just to be with my brother
and me. When you're fifteen, your dad can do that kind of stuff. He
can take off work whenever you need him to film your movie. But by
the time you're twenty-three, you realize that he'll pay for that later,
mostly by not sleeping and training new salesmen for free.

*Sierra Street* was based on a series of books my dad read to me as
a kid about three kids who have a detective agency and solve crimes.
It was probably cool for him to relive that with me, in the place
where he first read those stories. We even had his two best childhood
friends, Mike Escobar and Bob Badal, act in the film. Mike played a
robber and Bob a crooked cop. If you knew these guys, you'd laugh
at that part. I don't know how you get more nostalgic than that. My
dad smiled a lot on those days. The kind of smile you don't need to
show teeth for.

And now he wanted to be a part of my trip to South Korea. It
was time to reunite father and son for the sake of great cinema.

Instead, I say this: "Dad, you don't know anything about making films. Why would I take you?"

Sometimes, in writing books, you have to just guess at the things
you half remember. You have to half make up things you said so
people can get the idea. But this is verbatim.

I left for South Korea on tense terms with my father. But that was me at the time. I was the rebel filmmaker. The Steve Jobs of cinema. I marveled at Jobs's creativity, and I marveled at his stick-it-to-the-man disobedience. I wanted to wear jeans when everybody else wore suits, and my dad wasn't the hip young visionary in product development; he was the stiff in sales.

In keeping with the Jobs analogy, my dad was actually a lot like Steve Wozniak, Jobs's best friend, who seemingly just wanted to do something cool with his friends (in my dad's case, his son). I was condescending toward my dad in the same way Jobs was toward Wozniak. I always talked down to him, and I thought I would be the one to show him how to love a woman or what it looked like to really live life.

It was best that he stayed behind. He'd learn more that way, I reasoned. By watching me do what I was made to do. By watching me live the dream.

So on December 15, 2011, Dad got up early to drive Kevin and me to the airport for the greatest adventure of our lives.

Chapter 7

# THE BOX FOR BABIES

*What difference do you think you can make,*
*one man in all this madness?*

Edward, *The Thin Red Line*

On December 15, 2011, the day my team and I were to assemble
and fly to South Korea, I woke up early—sleepy, but pulsating with
excitement and nerves and fear. In secret, I dreaded the flight over
and had been convinced since I saw *Vertigo* in my Hitchcock course
that I had, well, vertigo. I took my last shower and had my last shave,
planning to grow a beard while shooting a film overseas like Francis
Ford Coppola would in Vietnam. Stopping at the door, I put on my
ball cap and jacket, cracked my knuckles, and caught my profile in
the mirror. Cheeks red and pitted, I turned and stepped out briskly
toward parts unknown.

When you're leaving on a trip like this, you notice things you've
never noticed before—the way the sun hits buildings in the early
morning, the way the car smells, and how you get to live by the
beach while most of the world has to settle for lakes. Your awareness of things is heightened, as taking a huge group of kids on an
international flight is only slightly different from going into a battle.

In the airport we were misfits. We were, it finally occurred to
me, like the groups of kids from all of the movies I loved growing up,
totally unequipped to do what we were about to do, but somehow
going to do it anyway. Just a bunch of cold, scared kids in the clothes

our parents bought us. Around me stood people whose company I loved and people I hardly knew, like my brother.

Sterling gripped her monopod like a ski pole atop a black diamond run. She loved documentaries, but maybe not making documentaries.

Bryce had his guitar because I forced him to bring it. Part of the reason being I wanted him to write songs in the film's place of origin, influenced by the sights, smells, and tastes of actual South Korean culture. More of the reason being I thought he sounded like Jeff Buckley, and "Hallelujah" was the closest I got to Christian music.

Mitch liked to monologue and he was already talking about a documentary "squeakquel" featuring songs by Alvin and The Chipmunks. He'd been with me since the early days and was wearing the director's hat I once gave him with an Oscar statue looming above the bill. In an eighties movie, he'd be the Corey Haim to Bryce's Corey Feldman. Will would be the Emilio Estevez character (the jock) in *The Breakfast Club*, and I would be Molly Ringwald in any of her films.

To make matters worse, TSA agents stopped us in the security lane straightaway, thinking our RED Camera was an explosive. No joke. I was so angry. I couldn't believe it. I mouthed off to the women inspecting my bag. I checked the time, checked the departure board, generally exasperated. It sent me into a quiet rage. The kind that everyone on the crew notices straightaway. These are the moments when you miss your parents for the first time. The moments when you would normally check your phone while they clean up the mess you've made.

Once I finally came through security and settled into my seat, I browsed through the movie selections on the headrest screen in front of me. Movies had always calmed me, even taken care of me.

As the plane rattled and jerked down the runway, I prayed that we'd all make it there and back again. Like the hobbits did. I also shortly realized that Korean Air was the cushiest airline in existence. Shayan, Sam, and I were quickly handed slippers and cucumber face towels.

Seoul is the capital city of South Korea. But based on my photo searches, it looked a lot like America, splattered with shopping malls, high-rises, and neon lights. Then there was the orphanage, the little hut in a concrete jungle. Sitting between Sam and Shayan (both conked out on Ambien) I juggled directorial ideas in my head, thumbing through all the Wikipedia pages I had printed out describing Korean history over the past six hundred to seven hundred years. In my binder I also carried film releases, location releases, and interview questions, most of them to do with plastic surgery.

1. What is your name?

2. Is South Korea the plastic surgery capital of the world?

3. When did plastic surgery become popular in South Korea?

4. How many clinics are there in Seoul? In South Korea?

5. Is there anything we did not cover in the
above questions that you would like to discuss?

Before the trip began, it's important to say that our film was
entirely centered on themes like this: "A man rescues poor, disabled,
and deformed babies in the plastic surgery capital of the world."
Sounded pretty film festival worthy to me and pretty compelling to
everybody else. We were making a film that happened to be about
a pastor, but it could have been about anyone. An infertile butcher
would have been interesting, for example, or maybe a swarthy drifter
who had run over a child by accident six years ago and was now
saving babies as a way of paying penance.

That would have gotten us a nomination. But alas, we were left
with the "mailbox for unwanted babies" concept. Not too shabby.
Even if the pastor guy ended up being some sort of mad baby collector,
we were gonna come out of this with an incendiary social-issue piece,
perfect for Netflix and a premiere at the ArcLight in Hollywood.

Unbeknownst to some of the crew, I had also purchased and
planned to plant a surveillance camera either inside the drop box
itself or within the house to capture a potential drop-off. If that
sounds unethical to you, don't worry, it never happened. But the
hope was to be in the orphanage in the dead of night when the alarm
bell rang and then quickly boot up the cameras just in time to follow our hero down the stairs and into the laundry room (where the
box was). We didn't know how he had built the box yet, or whether
building it in the first place was legal, but we did know a bunch of
kids from the American suburbs wasn't exactly the South Korean
government's international news team of choice.

Not unlike most people who heard the story, what wooed me about it all was that this man had built something symbolic. He had drawn a line in the sand and said, "No one dies here, not in my neighborhood." Something about that got into my bones the way filmmaking did in my old haunts. Something like courage. Real courage, the kind you want to see in your dad. The pastor had built a bunker for babies and was defending it with his entire life.

Before we left, a lot of people told me I had a savior complex, that I was engaging in the modern-day white man's burden. And in some way they were right. I didn't want to make a documentary in America, about pedestrian domestic issues. I knew it wasn't as cinematically sexy to film a documentary on skid row about abandoned babies. I knew it wasn't cool enough or trendy enough to fly to New Jersey to spin some yarn about single mothers in crisis. It had to be daring. It had to be adventurous. It had to be exotic.

But I really didn't have a savior complex. Trust me, I just had a Sundance complex.

*This is a facility for the protection of life. If you can't take care of your disabled babies, don't throw them away or leave them on the street. Bring them here.*
Inscribed on orphanage door

We were eleven fresh-faced, North Face-wearing, SoCal kids who had just gotten off an airplane in one of the biggest, most chaotic, and crowded cities in the world. It was more apparent than ever that some of the kids on our film crew hadn't even graduated from high school yet. Words were flying at us, rapid-fire, in a different language. We had a name, a phone number, an invitation, and an address but no way to get there and no guarantee we could really capture what was happening.

There's a lot on the line when you put eleven students on an airplane bound for a foreign country where you'll be spending other people's money on a gut feeling. I was terrified, but people probably thought I was just cold.

It was going to be my first Christmas away from family, and sensory overload ensued within seconds of stepping into the city. As I surveyed the colorful buildings before me from a high bridge, I spotted about ten to fifteen big white crosses planted on rooftops across the sprawling city. In a desperate attempt to communicate with the world around me, even just symbolically, I took the cross necklace from inside my T-shirt and let it fall down my outermost layer. Putting on another coat, I asked Shayan about the cameras and if they'd still run in the bitter cold.

"Shayan," I fretted, "these cameras cost more than my first year in film school."

Straightaway, Sam shimmied us into cabs and started quarreling with the lead driver. Squished five across in the backseat of a heated car and wrapped in snow gear, I was ready for us to move. Sam pointed to the address on the paper multiple times, and the driver waved his hand to and fro, clearly against the proposition. It immediately reminded me of those scenes in movies where the protagonist unknowingly reads the driver an address to a haunted mansion and watches the driver's eyes go wide and his face sheet white. After a few more rounds of Sam's broken-Korean beggary, he somehow convinced the driver to take us to the Gwanak-gu district. The city appeared like something you'd make out of Legos if you had lost the instruction manual. Mismatched oranges, greens, and blues, crowds of commuters in loud designer clothes, and coffeehouses built one on top of the other.

As the rickety cab loped through the streets of one of South Korea's poorest districts, I was suddenly aware that our driver was also watching television while he swerved through narrow lanes of traffic. As we careened around the corner and banked up a hill lined with vocal street marketers selling their wares to people on bicycles, my stomach started to churn. I was feeling like I did when I started high school.

I suddenly understood why the driver was hesitant, as the car tipped backward like a roller coaster clicking to the top of the track. It was the steepest hill I'd ever driven up, and the pastor was supposed to live somewhere near the top.

As we climbed, kids in private-school uniforms whizzed by our windows, too close for comfort, and pizza-delivery motorcycles sputtered and hissed out in front of the cab. Sam pointed up to the right and I caught a glimpse of another big white cross atop a nearly sideways powder-blue house.

As I realized exactly what I was seeing, my heart started to catch up with the rest of my body. To this day, I've never felt the same feeling of arrival as I felt at that moment, when the driver and us kids all parked in front of a long set of stairs leading to the box for babies.

"We're actually here," I said. "It's not just a photo anymore."

Inside, behind the door, were the noises, smells, and chaos of a working orphanage. Toys strewn about the floor and a puzzle-piece carpet laid out over the hardwood. Then there was the room where the drop box babies go. We could hear only crying from in there. I went to the door, as if to open and peek, but someone nearby uttered a disturbed "no" before I could turn the knob. I opted to try again when no one was watching. Bottles everywhere, still slick with milk. Stacks of paper and the miles of red tape and bureaucracy that come with the literal transfer of one human life from an anonymous entity to a man with a name and a purpose:

Pastor Lee.

We decided not to bring the cameras into Pastor Lee's house, initially. The idea was to just share a meal together first and not bring a bunch of fancy Hollywood machines into the room. There would be plenty of time for that later. I knew, because I had the experience planned and choreographed it down to the minute. The truth is that documentary films are barely more real than regular dramatic films. It's a weird sensation to fly somewhere and put people's lives on your hard drives, but that was the agreement. And it was just fine with me. As long as they would listen and obey, I could get some really great moments out of them, I thought.

The truth is that I had an agenda even for that meal. While I wanted to get information—about Pastor Lee, about his goals for the film, and so on—they just wanted to share a meal with some new friends. I grew impatient but was crippled by the language barrier. Jin had to do all the talking.

In South Korea you always take your shoes off when you enter a home, which you can imagine becomes something of a nightmare for a bunch of kids wearing combat boots (even though we've never seen actual combat). Once we all got our shoes off, we sat on the floor around several tables that had been pushed together. The meal was some kind of soup—a smelly bean soup with rice—and a side of droopy, sour cabbage (otherwise known as kimchi). The meal itself was an exercise in chaos. There were orphanage kids, many of them with disabilities, climbing all over the place and all over each other. My mind drifted to the time my professor told the class to avoid two things above all else when making your first student film: "Little kids and animals."

I scanned the room for pets.

Korean living is so communal. Pastor Lee and his wife had at least four children in their room each night. Privacy was just a pipe dream there. I thought about how much of my life I spent alone watching movies. That kind of life would be unfathomable for Pastor Lee.

Finally, I had a chance to ask Pastor Lee what he wanted to accomplish with the film.

"I don't want it to be about me," he declared through an interpreter. "It needs to be about saving lives."

Needless to say, this presented something of a problem for me. Pastor Lee *was* my movie. He was my star.

"So in the spring of May 2009, it was a cold and windy night," he began. "Someone left a baby around 3:00 a.m. The father of the baby, fortunately, called us at three. 'I'm sorry. I can't take care of the baby. I put the baby in front of your gate. Please, Pastor, take care of the baby. I'm sorry, but please.' So I ran out to the gate immediately, and the baby was in a paper box wearing thin clothes. There was one bottle and five diapers. The baby looked newly born, and she wasn't even cleaned up yet. I cried once I saw the baby. There was a stray cat passing by that night."

All I could picture was Robin Williams as baby Peter Pan in *Hook,* lying in the rain. The cat would have to be Tinker Bell.

"We thought about setting up a small room," Pastor Lee confided. "Then we could at least provide protection against stray cats. But we couldn't think of where to prepare the room. The parking garage was the only available space, but it was barely enough for our van. We then thought about placing a wooden box outside. We didn't need much room to place a box, and it could be as small as a baby's body. We could cover it to keep the baby from rain and snow. But the box reminded us of a coffin."

*Coffins are good*, I thought to myself. People like scary.

"Six months later, I read an article about a baby box in the Czech Republic," he said. "So we sent an email to the hospital in the Czech Republic. 'Can you teach us how to make it?' We sent four emails but never received a reply ..."

Sounded like me trying to reach South Korea.

"… and then we heard the news that an abandoned baby body was found in South Korea. It was getting cold in December. So I asked my friend, an iron worker, to make the baby box with the measurements I gave him. I fixed up what he made and put the box where it is now. I prayed that no babies would have to come. Two months later, in February 2010, a baby came in at 2:40 in the afternoon. There were many spectators, so I thought of not going down. But I thought, no, I should go check. And there was the baby, with its umbilical cord tied with a string. Tied loosely. I think he was born from an unwed mother inside a house."

Hunched over the low table, I listened to Jin translate how Pastor Lee named the first baby Moses because the actual Moses was found floating down a river in a reed box. I had never heard about Moses as a baby before, but I thought that was cinematic.

"He also said the baby looked handsome," concluded Jin.

And with a soft smile, the first interview was over.

After the conversation with Pastor Lee, Will and I went to see the drop box itself, lodged into the eastern wall of Pastor Lee's three-story lean-to.

"Bring them here," I remembered. "Bring them here."

This was the place where thirty-eight babies had been left forever, never to know where they started or whether their parents had dropped them off out of pure love or pure desperation—or both. At the time, I didn't know what it was like not to know my parents.

But in another sense, I totally did. I had made myself some kind of orphan.

When I finally walked up the concrete steps to the alleyway where the box was, I saw it, the hatch that had haunted me since June.

But, to my disappointment, and much like seeing the Grand Canyon, this moment came and went really, really fast. As my dad had said on the way to the Grand Canyon a few years before, "Prepare to be underwhelmed!"

The drop box itself looked industrial and utilitarian—like the oven door in a restaurant kitchen. Thousands of people probably walked or drove by the drop box every day without wondering or caring why there was a metal door with a little red light nearby. Most people probably thought it was for canned food or old clothes. I beckoned for Sterling to scurry over and start taking some photos for the travel blog.

But as Will stood next to me and faced the box, his eyes never left center field. I could see in his eyes a compulsion to open the door, the same kind kids have to open closets in the dark. The brittle and frightened longing to make sure no monsters are lying in wait for you to close your eyes. It's always about feeling safe.

I thought about the women who had come to this box to leave their children forever and how the babies would lie in that box in the dark, like a second womb. My film teacher once told us that movies could bring us back to the womb in some way, to a place we felt safe. To a place where nothing bad could happen to us. That's how it felt to make movies when all we made was *The Lord of the Rings*. We weren't making art. Please. That's one of the most dangerous

things you can do. We didn't make movies in forests with investors
for audiences; we made movies in manicured thickets with friends
for family. There weren't even mosquitoes where we lived. It was safe
because sometimes we didn't even go outside. We just pretended the
stairs were mountains and the room with a fireplace was the great
hall. It was safe because no one felt the burden of finishing on time
or proving himself.

And I think everyone wants to feel that way, not just about making something, but about being something. Everyone wants to feel
like there's a safe place to be useless at stuff and average at other stuff.
When we don't feel safe, we hide under the covers. In some ways,
when we don't feel safe anymore, we become the movie, the thing
that looks real but actually isn't.

Maybe Will was thinking the same thing about Pastor Lee's
contraption.

□

When you open the box, an alarm goes off in the house upstairs. So
after Will turned the handle for the first time, I worried that we'd just
sent the whole place into red alert. Will felt around inside, touching
the pressure sensor and the ratty yellow blanket at the bottom.

But as I stared through the box, into the laundry room behind it,
all I could think about was how I planned to film the opening scene,
where the hooded girl creeps into the alley, just like I wrote it in my
head. And I knew it was going to be fun too, a lot like the old days.
Shayan, Mitch, and I would stake out the box with binoculars and

Korean pastries, keeping watch for a teenage mom, cradling a child in swaddling clothes. On our cue, Pastor Lee would enter, frame right, with a Bible in his left hand and a baby bottle in his right and, of course, make a clean exit. Aaaaaaand cut!

Print that, baby. Let's tell the whole world!

After all, these were the most helpless kids in the nation. Somebody had to broadcast their plight, right? Their only shot was getting saved, and in my head at the time, I had the chance to tell one of the most high-stakes stories available.

But for Will, the adventure had clearly stopped, much like an old wrecked VHS tape. In his face, there was nothing but sadness. Not like when USC would lose football games sadness; I mean actual, deep-in-the-gut sorrow. It was almost like Will could picture himself inside that box, inside that little wooden womb. Just a helpless kid, waiting to be found.

I closed the hatch with a shrug.

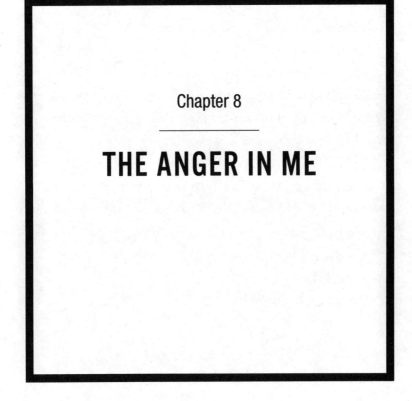

Chapter 8

# THE ANGER IN ME

*Quentin: They watched us get arrested. We're practically*
*ex-convicts. They'll never dance with us.*
*O'Dell: Quentin, you don't know anything about women.*

*October Sky*

Like Chris Tucker to Jackie Chan, my baby brother began our second interview by relaying loud, punctuated instructions to Pastor Lee. Sweating like a nurse, Kevin finally managed to tape the pastor's lapel mic down and out of sight. While he strapped on the sound gear, Shayan and Mitch set up the cameras, and I ordered everyone else around.

I was the genius with a thousand helpers.

Leaning back against an old family chair, sprightly Pastor Lee had a real smile on his face, the kind that took over his face. He wore a hanbok (traditional Korean garb), socks, sandals, and slim-rimmed grandpa glasses. I was automatically thankful for how charming he appeared on camera. He was the perfect lead. Humble, unassuming, and had great teeth. It would be easy for the audience to relate to him and also look up to him when he did all the brave stuff.

We arranged the lights and fired up the RED cameras, and Jin began prepping Pastor Lee on our interview goals. Mainly, we just wanted to understand how this box had come to be and who it had saved.

It's a weird thing to direct a movie blind. All you can do is come up with questions and hope your translator is actually asking them.

In order to avoid interrupting the flow of emotional interviews, Jin
or Sam would essentially translate back to me interview summaries,
which were for all intents and purposes really unhelpful versions of
whatever was just said. For all I knew, they were talking about baseball.

Here's an example of how this system usually worked:

"Jin, can you please ask the venerable pastor about his motiva-
tion for building this box for unwanted babies?" I would ask.

"Yes, sir," Jin would reply buoyantly.

*Pastor Lee answers for thirteen to fifteen straight minutes. Jin clears
his throat to summarize for me.*

"He said it was God's idea."

"Super."

This continued for fifteen days.

But on December 16, sitting behind my translator (Jin), I began
to see a man I didn't expect. Behind the perfect teeth and the dis-
tinguished salt-and-pepper hair, I met a man who spent most of his
twenties drunk, who played guitar as a way of chasing skirts, and was
generally kind of an angry jerk. I, of course, saw no parallels between
our lives whatsoever.

"Well," he would say with a Jimmy Stewart side-mouthed grin,
"girls used to follow me."

It was not the kind of interview I expected from a pastor. It was
rich with life and death and love and misery and failure and sex and
abortion and booze and Saint Augustine and bare-knuckle boxing.
The man was a walking, talking Coen brothers movie. But to be honest, he didn't buck the trend for me either. I had heard these kinds
of stories from Will and Bryce and other Christian men and women
that intersected with my journey to the other side of the world. I had

heard these kinds of stories in CRU every single week. Authenticity actually seemed to be the trend for young (and now old) Christians I met during that time of my life, nothing like the movies or the news would tell me before I actually started to search out stories for myself.

All the news media showed were Christians who had cheated on their wives or embezzled money from their flock. But these stories were different. They were stories of people who did all those terrible things until God got hold of their lives and rewrote the narrative.

Oh, and just because I know you were probably wondering, here's the story of his bare-knuckle boxing, written how I imagined it in my head.

Scene 1: We find ourselves at the Korean Spring Festival. It's daytime. Pastor (not yet) Jong-rak Lee staggers through the crowd at Korea's Samjinnal, or spring-opening festival, wasted on Azalea wine.

Kids play Korean games all around.

**Jong-rak:** (under his breath) Stupid kids.

The little rapscallions SNICKER and throw rice cakes at the drunken Jong-rak.

**Jong-rak (continued):** Hey! You brats! Ouch!

Jong-rak DRUNKENLY GRASPS at the children, but they're too fast for his slow-mo swings. He chases them into the crowd, but they evade him like a schoolyard game.

After a few more feeble slugs, Jong-rak's fist accidentally and POWERFULLY CONNECTS with the stomach of a random passerby, who just happens to be his BOSS.

Jong-rak's new boss, in his forties, is about a head taller than him and is clearly perturbed by the misplaced punch.

The kids SCATTER.

> **Rapscallion:** Fight! Fight! Fight!

> **Jong-rak:** Sorry, pal, you need to watch where you're going!

> **Boss:** ME?! (Beat) Hey, don't you work for me?

> **Jong-rak:** No, I think you work for me! I own a factory.

> **Boss:** You're drunk!

> **Jong-rak:** You're drunk!

Dozens of festivalgoers gather and encircle the two plastered boxers.

> **Boss:** You're Jong-rak!

> **Jong-rak:** You're Jong-rak! No.

**Boss:** You're dead.

**Jong-rak:** I'm not afraid of you, buddy boy. Put 'em up.

A few of Jong-rak's closest coworkers DASH through the crowd and WEDGE their way to the inner ring of the circle.

**Friend:** You can do it, Lightning!

**Friend 2:** Do the high kick! Do it, Jong-rak!

**Friend 3:** Jong-rak, if you die, I would like your watch!

*At this juncture, it's important to note that I am not making this up. Pastor Lee was actually known throughout the factory as Lightning because he was very fast and had a very impressive high kick.*

**Random Guy:** My bet's on the skinny kid!

*He was also as skinny as a Korean flute. (Which he still plays. Poorly.)*

**Boss:** Do you know where this body's been?

**Jong-rak:** No. And don't call me "Ben."

With the speed of drunken lightning, Jong-rak LURCHES at his boss, who DODGES the first KICK by somersaulting into a woman making soybean paste. Jong-rak LEAPFROGS off the bean cart and LANDS DIRECTLY ON TOP OF THE MAN, now hugging his neck like Cary Elwes hugged Andre the Giant in *The Princess Bride*.

The boss grabs Jong-rak by both arms and HURLS him into the dirt, where both ribs go CRACK-SLAM, and the whole crowd goes "OH MAN." Before he can get up, the boss SMASHES his foot into Jong-rak's ear. He'll feel that in the morning.

SPINNING AWAY, Jong-rak somehow rises to his feet and MOTIONS his opponent to CHARGE like a matador tempting a bull, blood now pouring from his broken eardrum.

Taking the invitation with pleasure, the menacing man CAREENS toward Jong-rak, who HIGH KICKS his new boss in the mouth, sending him REELING back into the arms of several young women, who are now undressing the victorious Jong-rak with their eyes.

SLOW FADE.

*Three weeks later, the president of the factory would finally leave the hospital, and Jong-rak would be fired for fighting for the third straight time.*

What I didn't process in the moment, but did later on, was that this was actually a really sad story. People laugh at drunks in movies, but in real life they're not so funny at all. Truth was, whenever Pastor Lee lost his job, his wife and daughter were also losing things. This man had a temper and, for whatever reason, wasn't ashamed to tell us about it. But it didn't seem like he was bragging either. He just felt free from trying to keep it all under wraps.

It was then that I started to think about how I had screamed at my girlfriend back home. It's one thing to scream at the guy trying to kick your eardrum; it's another to scream at the person you're supposed to cuddle with and adore. Most people probably didn't see the anger in me back in Orange County, just like they don't see most problems people have in places like that. They're under cover. They're behind closed doors. If fights break out, they break out on private streets, in gated communities.

"At least I never hit anyone," I convinced myself. "At least I never hit her. I'm not like that."

I kept that part of me gated.

◻

Stepping into the orphanage director's office, a motherly woman ushered me to a small desktop computer, surrounded by photos of the kids tucked into soft-cover albums with stickers maniacally applied to every side. By all accounts, she was the "house mom," and even amidst the daily slog, she looked like her name: Young. Catching pieces of English with childlike glee, Young started burrowing through computer files and showing me different folders with weird and long Korean symbols in front of them. Everyone was busy at the time, except Shayan and me. We had asked her if she had any photos of babies who had been dropped off in the box, since we hadn't seen one for ourselves.

She nodded like she may have had something somewhere but wasn't sure and had to look.

I glanced at Shayan and said, "Whatever she has is fine. I'm sure we'll catch a live one on camera while we're here."

Then, very casually, Young clicked on a folder, and dozens of little MP4 video files dropped down like the puck on a carnival strength tester. They couldn't all be …

… Yep, they were all videos. We had struck justice-movie/baby-movie gold.

They had filmed every single drop-off to date.

Chapter 9

---

# PAINFULLY AND CONSCIOUSLY SELF-AWARE: MAKING MOVIES

*Of course I have a secret identity. I don't know a single superhero who doesn't. Who wants the pressure of being super all the time?*

Mr. Incredible, *The Incredibles*

The best cheeseburger I ever had was in South Korea.

Ever since I saw Morgan Spurlock's *Super Size Me* back in 2004 (admittedly one of the few docs I'd seen before making my own), I gave up on Mickey D's for good. In SoCal, there was something noble about eating In-N-Out only on road trips anyway. So when I went to South Korea, the last thing on my mind was, "Hey, Sam, can you ask our impoverished hosts to buy me a Big Mac? I don't really care for what their volunteer cook whipped up this afternoon."

Maybe hiding my helping of kimchi in the potted plants was a dead giveaway, or maybe it was how my face looked when I pretended to slurp the soup. Either way, in South Korea, I had my first Big Mac in eight years and it was transcendent. Usually, I didn't need to stop shooting to eat, but when that missionary dropped three greasy brown bags on the table, next to all that seaweed and cabbage, all bets were off. I needed something—anything—that tasted like home.

I'm often asked if this experience was one of those fun, team-and-camaraderie-building trips that people tend to romanticize after the fact. Make no mistake about it. It was miserable.

I think most people have this mental picture of filmmaking as magical and glamorous, where the director sits in an elevated chair behind a Panavision camera. He's barking orders good-naturedly through a bullhorn, and Matt Damon is boyishly laughing in between really strong takes. The director's face has just the right amount of masculine stubble, and the ball cap he wears is emblazoned with the logo of his last hit movie.

But making *The Drop Box* in South Korea was the kind of activity that made you want to stop and eat fast food. To start with, we probably slept only two or three hours per night, which was partly a result of wanting to stay up and be prepared for if and when a baby was left in the box. More realistically, it had to do with the fact that there were nine people crammed into an unfurnished apartment near the orphanage. We all shared a bathroom. I slept on the floor each night, surrounded by hard drives (we brought twenty-four), camera cords, and rechargeable batteries. I looked like something from *The Matrix* curled up amid all the cords.

We'd also never shot on these cameras before, and there was a lot of learning on the fly. In a documentary like this, you can't ask the caregiver to carry the crippled child down the stairs a second time because you didn't get the shot the first time. You've got one shot and you'd better land your focus, or you could miss a moment that makes the movie work. It's unsettling, to say the least.

It also occurred to me that if just one small wire on the camera were to break, there would be no replacing it in South Korea, and the movie would grind to a halt. Once, Mitch caught me cleaning a five-thousand-dollar RED camera lens with the sleeve of my fleece jacket, which (I was later told) could irreparably scratch it. Mitch didn't say a word. It's one of the strange dynamics that happens on a film shoot. Because it was "my" movie, people were sometimes afraid to tell me when I was doing something dumb. The fact of the matter is, I collected hard drives full of unusable footage that I hoped no one would ever see.

You have to understand, up to this point I had made movies essentially on my own. I was my own chief cook and bottle washer. I wrote, directed, designed, produced, and edited every little film I made. In the beginning, most of that was out of necessity, but eventually it was out of insecurity. I delayed adulthood, so to speak, as a filmmaker by surrounding myself only with people I could control, who would defer to me to make decisions. That way, when I did make an error, it was a safe place to fail.

The shadow mission of building a team of nonfilmmakers was that I surrounded myself with ignorance to appear enlightened. No one would think to question my authority, because they knew even less than me, just by default. I even subordinated people like Sterling (the only other film major) so that she wouldn't question my directorial genius.

On the way to one of the interviews, all of us were packed into the sprinter van. Everyone was talking about flights and movies and random things. I was the only one not talking, which was rare. Anyway, I was sort of sprawled across the backseat, supposedly unaware of Sterling's behind-the-scenes camera. But in reality I was very aware. Conscious or not, I was making these sort of James Dean-ish overtures toward the camera. Doing stuff with my hair and basically being painfully and consciously self-aware.

My favorite moments were the quiet moments when I took the Scarlet out into the neighborhood at night, all alone, where I could be totally incompetent with the tripod and the five-thousand-dollar lenses and the same camera Peter Jackson was using in New Zealand. I could breathe again, without anyone breathing down my neck. Just me and the camera and the kid in me. I could be naked in those moments. I knew myself. I knew my limits, and I wasn't going to tell myself "I suck." At night, amid the Christmas trees, I could safely admit I didn't know some terms Mitch was using. I could admit that I didn't understand how to use the toggles on the sound mixer and that I had forgotten to bring some essential parts to the Steadicam. I could come clean about having watched YouTube clips to understand most of what we were doing there.

I continued to spend a lot of time wandering the streets of Seoul by myself, with my camera, every night. I was looking for great shots (always), but really I was just using the time to be alone and pray/reflect/cuss/lust. Whatever you do out of sight. On these nighttime walks there were no expectations of me as the director. There were just lots of Christmas trees and a burning desire to make movies the way we did before our movies had to be any good.

Because even as the director, I didn't know whether this was going to work, whether we could capture the essence. I was just the kid who watched at least three movies every weekend, all alone, and prayed no one would show up like that stupid jerk kid at fifteen who told me to leave filmmaking to the smart people.

When no one was watching, that was the best.

When no one was watching, I could just be me.

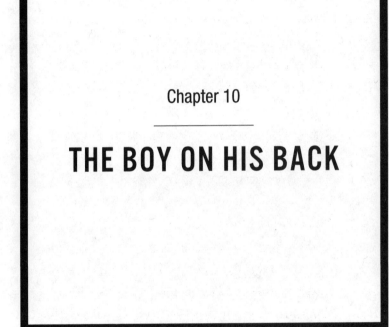

Chapter 10

# THE BOY ON HIS BACK

*When my son was born healthy, I never asked why. Why was
I so lucky? What did I do to deserve this perfect child, this
perfect life? But when he got sick, you can bet I asked why!
I demanded to know why! Why was this happening?*

Mrs. Lowe, *Awakenings*

After a few days of formal interviews, Pastor Lee invited us to meet
his only biological son, who had spent the majority of his life—
twenty-seven years—on his back.

He'd spent fourteen of those years living in and out of a hospital.
When I met him, I didn't know what to do or where to look. Pastor
Lee's wife, the boy's mother, was wiping gunk off his feeding tube. It
was an unspeakably uncomfortable moment, but I began to understand why this type of love felt real.

She had spent so many moments, so many hours, and so many
days by his bed—and had done so joyfully. I didn't understand, at
the time, how this was possible. Grinning from ear to ear, Mrs. Lee
grabbed my biceps, jokingly, and said they were "skinnier than the
bedposts." She had a joy and a sense of humor that went beyond the
language barrier. I wished that I could smile like that while changing
a grown man's diaper.

As we stood by the boy who had lived life on his back, Pastor
Lee's wife started to sense our awkwardness. Earnestly, she looked at
us and said, "He'd be a lot happier if you were girls."

□

Outside Pastor Lee's orphanage, all the children were just collections of flawed DNA with barely beating hearts. Inside, they were all stories—archived and documented for us in soft-cover photo albums and chipped wood frames all over the walls. Outside, they were forgotten, but inside they each had a name—like Autumn, a young girl who was left in the box in the fall, and a little boy named Victory with cheeks that inflated when he smiled.

And then there was Eun-man, translated as "full of God's grace."

Problem was, although he was called "the boy on his back," he was really a man. A man, technically brain-dead, who had spent the entirety of his life being cared for around the clock. Eun-man was fed through a tube in his neck—a wound that had to be cleaned and aspirated daily. He had to be stripped bare and bathed and dressed by a team of adults, since his parents couldn't even pick him up by themselves. His care alone, not to mention that of the other children in the orphanage, made moviemaking look like a hobby.

Pastor Lee and his wife slept in the room where Eun-man lay, along with three orphans with, essentially, the same condition. Those kids didn't breathe like normal; they just gargled their own phlegm all day long. Before filming, I even made a point to check for gargling because honestly it became hard to tell if they were dead or alive. Every night, Pastor Lee slept with one eye open, cognizant of the fact that at any time, Eun-man or one of the children could choke and that would be the end of it. It was unthinkable, especially since I usually slept in until eleven o'clock on Saturday mornings.

They called Eun-man's room "The Happy Room," partly as a rebellion against societal norms of what happiness is. Also, because against all logic and reason, there seemed to be happiness in that room—that room where the grimy, gritty, unlovely work of a caregiver was done.

There was a pain that only a full-time caregiver could know, and it was the reality that as you battle to keep one life viable, that battle is slowly whittling away at your own life and health. Pastor Lee, in particular, bore the scars, as he endured high blood pressure, diabetes, and his own weight loss. Outwardly, he seemed to be withering, but inwardly, I got the sense that we were the same age.

Seeing Eun-man, I was reminded of the wild disparity between what I had been experiencing and the pervading ethic in Hollywood. In Hollywood, your worth is measured by your looks and your production. It is the territory of beautiful, privileged, and accomplished people. The first question out of our mouths, about any actor or director, is, "What has he done?" In those situations, I am always tempted to say *Sierra Street*, just to mess with people, but all four parts are still on YouTube (reader, watch at your own risk).

Still, standing over Eun-man's bed, I debated about whether he was happy or even there. And if he was, maybe he was living his own personal nightmare inside his head. It wouldn't be fair to let that go on, I thought to myself. At some point, I resolved that Pastor Lee and his wife were keeping him alive for their own benefit. And hey, that was understandable. It would obviously be impossibly hard to say good-bye to their own child. Then again, what great benefit did Pastor Lee ever receive from Eun-man?

That was the main question I had back then.

There were chilling moments during the filming when we would be in the room with Eun-man, and Pastor Lee would ask him for a "million-dollar smile" for the camera. And for long, pregnant moments, Eun-man would just lie there. Like he always did.

So after the first meeting, believing Eun-man played no part in my grand narrative (he couldn't talk or even really emote), I ordered the team to set up interviews with anyone else of note.

In our first interview of the next day, the dad of a girl with Down syndrome started crying on camera. In the next, a mom told us how her disabled boy once attacked a helpless classmate with a pair of scissors. Safe to say, we were already getting great material. In my head, this was the kind of movie you just showed up for. The concept was good enough that all we had to do was be there, and the rest would take care of itself. After spending several days at the orphanage, I was honestly just excited to get out to where the action was. I anxiously calculated and rehearsed upcoming interviews with plastic surgeons and kids who had gotten nose jobs over Christmas break. With plenty of cute baby footage in tow, it was high time to start making juxtapositions between perfectionist Korean culture and the counterculture of this heroic pastor.

But no matter how far we traveled or how interesting the plastic surgeons were, I had the sneaking suspicion that God wanted to tell a different story. I had the inkling every time we came back to the orphanage that there was enough there. None of these people had fancy titles, but there was something like real life in that three-story lean-to. The budding director in me wanted to traverse the nation and uncover the deepest and darkest secrets of the Korean culture, pitting Pastor Lee against it. That was what I told everyone back home we were capturing.

But God kept bringing us back. Back to the room. Back to the bed of "the boy who wasn't there," as I called him.

"I went to morning break worship service for two years to pray for God to give me a son," Pastor Lee told us in the next interview. "When we went to the hospital to give a natural birth, my wife suffered labor pains. But they said the baby wasn't coming. I asked why and the doctor said that the face of the baby was too big."

While listening, I remembered the framed photo upstairs with a baby that looked like the guy in *The Elephant Man,* his cheek bulging out like a second head was growing from inside it.

"The doctor grabbed the baby and lifted him up. His face was malformed. I saw the whole labor scene," he said. "When I saw that, I wasn't able to thank God. I asked God why He had to give me that baby, not a healthy one. I unwittingly complained to God about it. But after thirty seconds, I repented. 'You gave me a son for my prayers and I was complaining.' I asked for forgiveness for my complaint."

I didn't know what repentance meant at the time, but it seemed like he had a good reason to be angry, or at least confused. I felt that way, too, about most of the movie I was making. It wasn't what

I hoped for, especially the interviews with Pastor Lee. Making this film felt like labor, and what came out was also something really deformed.

"So we went home. But after four months, his lymph became infected. It got scratched. It became a malignant tumor."

My mind zoomed upstairs and onto the face of Eun-man, the now-twisted remnant of a "scratch" (seriously?) that would leave him bedridden, brain-damaged, and incapable of even the most baseline human functions.

"The doctor told me to give up on my son because they did everything they could do. But I told them I wouldn't leave him like that because he was sent to us by God. However, because his breath had stopped before, oxygen couldn't get to the brain. His brain cells were all dead. Because of this, they said even if he's alive, he's just a vegetable. He wouldn't be able to do anything but lie on his back."

I wondered whether they ever thought of putting him out of his misery. He was, by a large margin, the most disabled of all of Lee's children. The way his face drooped, he looked a lot like Sloth from *The Goonies,* if Sloth hadn't been the one who saved the kids in the end but instead just festered in the Fratellis' basement, chained to the wall like in the beginning, when Mikey was afraid to look.

"There was a boy named Kim Il-gu, who had a brain tumor. Only a week was left for him to live," Pastor Lee recalled with a sigh. "I prayed for him and kept praying for him, without even praying for my own son. Eun-man was very sick then. But God saved the boy. Il-gu recovered and went home a week later. So I prayed for God to cure Eun-man as well. But He wouldn't. Because God used him on his back to save people."

The only reference point I had to something like this was my grandma Patricia. She had Alzheimer's and would sometimes get up in the middle of a meal and think she was at a train station or some other place and knock her silverware onto the tile. She forgot the names of her children and couldn't even use the bathroom on her own. It really killed me inside to see that. But that was my grandma. Eun-man didn't look like a cute little woman. He was harder to enjoy. And he hadn't been struck with his condition after living a normal life. He was for all intents and purposes always a needy, broken kid. I felt so sorry for him, but I didn't really spend much time around him. I preferred the other children. I wondered what it would be like to ever speak to Eun-man, and whether he'd chew me out for being so scared.

Feeling guilty, I began to see it as my duty as a rich kid from Orange County to help this family in whatever way I could. If nothing else, I felt compelled to leverage what I believed God had given me to make an impact on the lives of others. In that moment, I came to the conclusion that there are two kinds of people in this world: the helpless and the ones who help.

It wasn't until later that I'd find out which category of people I actually belonged to.

When I saw Pastor Lee in that room with his son, I saw somebody who wasn't faking it. There are "correct" responses for situations like these—you don't turn away in horror, you stay in the room, you dutifully serve, and so on. But Pastor Lee had a genuine love for his son that transcended duty. He wasn't just storing Eun-man until he died peacefully, probably somewhere between thirty and forty. And it was more than pity. More than "I feel bad." Pastor Lee genuinely liked Eun-man, even though his son would never and could never "do" anything for him, in the conventional sense.

Of course, you're saying, Pastor Lee has to love Eun-man. Even as a crooked kid, that's his son. There's a bond there that they're born with. Full-on rejection is possible but not at all probable. What I expected, though, was a frustrated love. A frustrated, strained, one-way relationship between a father and a difficult child. That's what I thought I would see.

But Pastor Lee didn't seem to just endure Eun-man.

He seemed to like him.

He seemed to like him a lot.

Chapter 11

# EVERYTHING BUT THE ILLUSION: CHRISTMAS

*I'm a god, I'm not The God … I don't think.*

Phil, *Groundhog Day*

It's really easy to love the kids who are cute. The kids who can offer you something back. The little boy with Down syndrome, for instance, he was popular with the whole crew. He danced to K-pop on the TV and would always take his pants off. Then there was the boy whose hand ended at the wrist. He peeled oranges and built Legos. But they both also enjoyed punching me and even punching the pastor. See, on day trips to sad places, it's all like babysitting. You want to take the kids home after it's over. But when you're living in their world for a while, the cutest kids do ugly things too. Like hurt you or hurt themselves. One of the cutest girls in the whole place slapped herself until her cheeks changed color. Another child screamed at Sarah and Sam.

Truth be told, I got annoyed by the kids as I was trying to make my self-proclaimed masterpiece. But my brother seemed to fare better. Since I had brought him only to hold the boom mic, he had a lot more free time than me. He always hung out with the kids who didn't have anyone else to hang out with. Like Sanghee, a girl who fell into a toilet when she was two and almost drowned. Or Nathan, the boy who drooled uncontrollably and laughed uncontrollably too.

*Maybe he related to them.*

□

On the morning of December 23, all but a few of us left for home to
be with family for Christmas. Soon it was just Sterling, Sam, Shayan,
and I. More than any of us, Sterling seemed to glow. She was a well-
to-do girl from Texas who had never done without, but she looked at
herself differently on those days. Christmas seemed like a big deal to
her. People called her by name and jumped all over her when she came
into the house. This wasn't weak-at-the-knees love. It was more.

For me, I gave very little thought to Christmas beyond how it
could serve the film. If I could be anywhere in the world I would be
making a movie. The way I had dreamed about it since I was small.
For the first time I got to make something, with a budget, that people
actually wanted to see. "There is no way I'm leaving this," I barked.
"There's no way I'm trading this in for some DVD stocking stuffers."

While most of my crew excitedly packed, high on the prospect
of flying home to the warm, loving embraces of family as well as the
excesses of an Orange County Christmas, I didn't want anything to
do with it. I rarely spoke to my parents while I was in South Korea,
save the initial "We made it. The plane didn't crash." In deep director
mode, I only scheduled a Skype session after Kim Jong Il died, and
that was only to reassure them we weren't on the brink of some kind
of nuclear holocaust.

I saw Christmas in South Korea as a way to break free from
the superficiality of an Orange County Christmas. The holiday
where people sat in the living room in their designer Minnetonka
Moccasins and slung presents at each other, pretending life was like

all the photos hung by the fridge. I wanted no part of it. I was thinking about Christmas as the season of love, joy, peace, and hope, but
was beginning to wonder if any of that was possible without God. I
saw a lot of those things on a day-to-day basis in the orphanage, with
Pastor Lee … so the last thing I wanted to do was go home just to be
reminded that America was more interested in Sharper Image.

Looking back, I was disillusioned with everything but the illu-
sion (film).

I had huge expectations for Christmas at the orphanage. If nothing
else, I figured it would completely trivialize commercial American
holidays. I was hoping and expecting that Christmas at the orphanage would be filled with prayer and none of the artifacts—fancy gifts,
gaudy decorations, banal chitchat, and so on—that made many of
my recent Christmases such shallow events.

The day started promisingly enough. As we were driving around
town it began to snow. Previously, Seoul had just been brutally cold,
with none of the fluffy white snow that makes Christmas such a
cinematic holiday.

Outside, the snow kissed the streetlights and the swing sets, hiding the city under a beautiful blanket of white. Inside, I was gearing
up for the most holy night ever.

At the orphanage, I asked Ruri, one of the older boys, what he thought about Santa Claus. "Santa Claus is dead," he responded. "He fell off the roof."

One for one.

Ruri has a beautiful story but is also an example of the kind of kid who can easily fall through the cracks in a setting like this because he's no longer young and cute. While volunteers and visitors love holding babies and playing with toddlers, Ruri's increasingly grown-up thoughts and interests can make it hard to connect. He's a middle school boy who is very close to becoming a man. He maintains eye contact and speaks like J. I. Packer trapped in a small Korean boy's body.

Because of his malformed hands, Ruri was ridiculed in school as a young boy, and as a result turned timid and withdrawn. But slowly his confidence grew as Pastor Lee gave his hands purpose.

"Don't you think God made your fingers that way?" Pastor Lee would tell him. "Don't you think God can use that?"

He also has unique insights into Pastor Lee's exhaustion. Because of the demands of running the orphanage, raising Eun-man, and being a de facto father to so many kids, it can be hard for him to have time for Ruri. But as a result, Ruri really fathers many of the other kids in the orphanage, which is, I'm sure, why he's so mature.

Maybe because I was self-absorbed, or maybe because it was too close for comfort, I saw some of myself in Ruri. The drive. The need for acceptance because we were both self-conscious about the way we looked. The fact that we both became student body presidents at our schools (he would serve a second term in fourth grade). Ruri is uniquely driven for a boy his age and hopes, one day, to be able to continue running the orphanage when Pastor Lee is no longer able. He helps in subtle but significant ways throughout the day: hanging laundry to dry, folding towels, changing diapers, rubbing Eun-man's back. He's the kind of kid you write about without trying to be puffed up, sarcastic, and clever.

He taught me how to sit next to Eun-man instead of stand over him. He also taught me that kids can pray and mean it, even if they haven't read a lot of Christian books. He's still teaching me.

☐

Christmas was The Big Day, the big scene, like Truman finding the door in *The Truman Show*. This was supposed to be, and was going to be, the big reveal—not only in the film but, I'd hoped, in my own heart. I was beginning to see how empty my life was, and I knew Lee and his clan of pastor's kids were about to commence the most devout day of the year.

I went through the itinerary in my mind:

5:00 a.m.: Everyone is up and praying together

8:00 a.m.: Everyone is still praying

9:00 a.m.–11:00 a.m.: Pastor Lee preaches a fiery sermon on how secular Christmas is actually Saturnalia (worship of the deity Saturn, otherwise known as Cronus)

11:00 a.m.–4:00 p.m.: Communion and quiet
reflection period

4:00 p.m.–7:00 p.m.: Gregorian chant

7:00 p.m.: Everyone gathers to hear the Christmas
story, as performed by Korean War orphans

This year there would be no iTunes gift cards, no Christmas
Eve church services so families could sleep in and enjoy Christmas
Day without the burden of God. No kids riding new Razor scoot-
ers in the street and then storing them in the garage for the rest of
the year.

I couldn't wait to show the world what God was really about.
What Christmas was really about. So I slapped a new battery on the
back of my Scarlet and crouched in the corner of the living room,
giving room for the Holy Spirit to move (or whatever Bryce would say
in Bible-speak).

Then, shortly after Ruri explained to me that Santa Claus had
fallen off the roof, the orphanage door burst open … and four tall
Santa Clauses—volunteers dressed in gilded holly-berry-red suits—
waddled into the house bearing enormous gifts.

I almost dropped the camera, all preconceptions shattered (they
brought clothes and shoes for the kids, by the way).

There was prayer that day, don't get me wrong. There was also
a service later in the day, and some corporate singing. But there was
also a ton of laughter. I thought about my parents then, and I hoped
they were thinking about me.

But what I remember most were the kids smiling because someone remembered them at Christmas. Maybe God's love wasn't too important to be there. Maybe it wanted to be there. That's what I remember. That's what I saw in their faces.

Just normal kids who knew they were made to be loved.

And when he received a present of his own, I even saw Eun-man, "The boy who wasn't there," smile.

Chapter 12

# THE MILLION-DOLLAR QUESTION

*I'm not bad. I'm just drawn that way.*

Jessica, *Who Framed Roger Rabbit*

Landing at the Bradley International Terminal at LAX does not mean you're home. What it means is you're still thirty minutes from customs and ninety minutes from all the people holding flowers from Ralph's. Before we got there, I imagined they were all waiting to greet me. I imagined the concourse lined with agents, producer reps, and distributors like Walden Media, the company behind *The Chronicles of Narnia*. Will would later inform me that those books were in some way not just about talking animals but also about biblical prophecies.

Of course, after we turned the corner, it was just our parents, the ones who had been watching us make movies since the start. My dad waved from the back, wearing jeans and running shoes like always. He teared up when he saw me, having had Kevin home safe for a week. Upon arriving home, I went upstairs to find my room covered with homecoming stuff. After all, my mom is the kind of mom who still pastes "Welcome Home, Son" onto purple construction paper. I thanked her and then took the most satisfying shower of my life.

In moments like that, you start imagining what it's like to never have "me time." To never have moments to yourself, except in the bathroom. I may have put in the hours overseas, but I always knew I was coming home. As much as I ridiculed the way my parents lived, I couldn't wait to see the ocean again.

I thought about how Pastor Lee lives in the mess every day of his life. He never has "me time." Everything he does and says is carried out in the presence of volunteers, extended family, and impressionable children.

After sleeping for sixteen hours straight, I went to my girlfriend's place. Partially satiated by her, I spent some time with my computer girlfriends too. In my spare time, I read the Bible. Before the trip, Will had given me advice on which Bible to buy, so I curled up on my girlfriend's couch with my NIV Study Bible and big black journal, ignoring all the parts about sex. I told my girlfriend about the trip and how hard it was. We talked in lovey-dovey baby voices when we were alone, the kind you use with your family pets. Finally, I could just be a kid again. I didn't have to be a leader or a big shot, just a boy, with all the normal hormonal felt needs. But somehow, it wasn't enough this time. It simply wasn't enough to be known in my pajamas by a nice girl.

Back at USC, I had Mitch build a computer to edit and store all the footage. He assured me he'd "done this before," the way a husband assures his wife during an emergency birth in the car on the way to the hospital that he's also "done this before." After Mitch was through tinkering with all the panels and pieces, he powered on the two-foot tower, and it blew the circuit to the entire north wing of the dorm.

At the time, I was halfway through my second year as resident adviser in the same dorms I started in at USC. Another way of delaying the idea of growing up. Still, it was a good deal since I didn't have to pay for meals and I had a whole room to myself. At least once a week, I blew the power to everyone's microwaves and laptops. I ruined a lot of hot pockets that semester. In that way, of course, I felt justified. Someone might have eaten those.

After I had skimmed through the footage for a few weeks, I realized that at some point all of this would need to be translated from Korean to English before it could become a story. Immediately, Sarah and Sam reached out to Korean clubs and organizations on campus. Enter Steve Kim, otherwise known as Scuba Steve.

### STEVE "SCUBA" KIM: TRANSLATOR/COPRODUCER

- Violinist
- Humanitarian
- Patriot
- Magician (no, really)

Steve essentially lived with me for several weeks in order to make sense of my movie. He worked for fifty dollars a day, and when I couldn't pay him right away he agreed to work for noodles. We developed a friendship I didn't expect. Before this, most of my filmmaking friends had been people exactly like Steve. Timid, portly, and skilled. They took orders from me and were obedient underlings. But this time, I was at the mercy of Steve's abilities. More than that, Steve seemed to be really affected by the footage, and I wondered why I never cried when Pastor Lee talked about burying a little girl named Hannah underneath the Christmas tree outside the house.

After Steve left, I essentially had twenty to thirty large slabs of marble I would need to carve into angels. Twenty to thirty interviews plus countless hours of B-roll that required shaping, and now I was alone in that and was doing the long-distance thing with the same girl from high school.

It wouldn't take long, while editing, for me to get supremely stressed and start itching for some sort of release.

While I was editing one sunny afternoon with the blinds closed, one of my residents knocked on the door. He was there to ask a question about intramurals or some other freshman activity, so I casually lifted the hood on my laptop to check out some schedules online. I clicked on the blue and red compass (Safari) in the bottom left corner of my taskbar, and the last page I visited popped into view. Looking over my shoulder, my resident eyed a bunch of little thumbnails, all featuring naked women in different positions and categorized according to their body types or colors. I offered a humiliated "What is this?" knowing full well what it was but fumbling to come up with an excuse that wouldn't change his perception of me. Respectfully, my resident left the room, offering to come back later.

I probably sat in that chair, hand hovering over the keyboard, for ten minutes. I wouldn't look at porn for a full month after that, the longest stretch in three or four years.

Back home, whatever normal release I was offered through my girlfriend was canceled out by an ugliness I couldn't fully explain. I looked up at the ceiling, as I had in so many different rooms and so many different places, and all I wanted was for it to feel good again, like it did when we were sixteen and seventeen. But it wouldn't. This wasn't the kind of guilt you feel after cutting somebody off on the 405. It was the kind that makes you sick. The kind that comes when you hurt somebody smaller than you or put somebody in the hospital when all you meant to do was put them in their place.

Back then, I thought about other women all the time. Lots of girls. Girls I saw in the dorms, girls from class, teachers, TAs, whoever I could remember. Whoever's voice I could remember and play back in my head, saying seductive things to me. Anything would turn me on. A gesture, a look, a waitress's accidental moan. I would wake up and go to class and go to bed thinking about different girls, even Christian girls I met. I took pictures with my eyes and then undressed the people in the pictures and put them in the zoetrope of my mind. Around and around they went, spinning and dipping and cooing. I was like the boy in the video rental store who sneaked behind the curtain into the adult section.

But at least I wasn't cheating, right? With self-righteous disgust, I looked down my nose at frat stars and guys in bro-tanks who joked about their latest extrarelational lay. I clung to that and continued to protect my girlfriend by keeping it all inside. To me at the time, everyone else was just getting through life whatever way they could. I didn't drink anymore and definitely didn't do drugs. According to my college health courses, I just had normal guy issues and needed to manage my bad behavior so it didn't leak into the lives of others.

I went to church and liked church more than I ever had in my whole life. I was going to CRU every week, and I even started journaling more about God and praying for Him to grant me self-control. I buckled down. I started to keep track of the days I went without sinning. Some weeks were better than others.

Still, when people would ask me questions about my faith, I didn't really know how to answer. They'd ask me to share my testimony, and I usually just talked about Will and South Korea and why I felt "called to go."

One night, I was sitting across from my friend Ben in his office, talking about God. At this point he was convinced I was a Christian because I'd told him I was and because I hadn't proven to be a huge hypocritical scumbag. Ben is the most well-spoken secular humanist on planet Earth. He was in my film production class and once made a film in Nova Scotia with horses and a train full of period-appropriate soldiers. I was in way over my head on several levels.

"In my heart of hearts, I just have doubts," he earnestly remarked.

"Doubt isn't the opposite of faith, you know? Sight is," I returned, thankfully remembering that quote from a local pastor.

"Where did you hear that?"

*Crap*, I thought in my head. *He's onto me.*

"What do you mean? I made it up," I replied indignantly.

*Lie.*

"Why don't you just say something original? Don't regurgitate. Something you really believe. I'd rather hear that. I really want to know. We're friends. Just tell me something from you."

"I am," I said sternly.

There was an awkward I-feel-trapped pause.

"Just tell me why," he chided.

"Why what?" I asked.

"Why you believe in Christianity. Why you're a Christian. Can't you tell me your story?"

*That was the million-dollar question.*

"Well," I said cautiously, "I had an, uh, experience. And, uh, when I went to the Bible I found experiences that were eerily similar."

*Huh?*

"Okay, eerily similar," Ben said, yawning. "That's good."

I had clearly converted him on the spot.

■

When people would ask me why God existed, I had answers in the chamber. I had listened to enough Ravi Zacharias debates to debunk subjective moral reasoning and enough John Lennox to know that Christianity wasn't a religion but rather a relationship with God. And like any relationship, I figured that God and I were just having normal ups and downs. I knew about the plans of God and the beautiful purposes God has for our lives. I knew about the goodness of God and the provision of God. I knew that God cared about me personally and that He was real. But when people would ask me about the cross, that's when I had to repeat somebody else's words.

On the first trip, I really flaunted my wooden cross necklace, you know, the one I bought on Amazon for eight dollars. Maybe I liked the idea of it. Maybe that's what it was worth to me.

When I left, I gave the cross necklace to Ruri to keep, and he still wears it every time I go to see him.

A few weeks after talking to Ben, when I finally understood the meaning, it made sense that I had left the necklace behind. We've all heard about the cross at one time or another. Some of us at church, others in the movies. But at some point, the cross can't just be something you buy on Amazon.

It has to be what bought you.

Chapter 13

# A MEAGER BUT REAL "I'M SORRY"

*Momma always said dyin' was a part of life. I sure wish it wasn't.*

Forrest, *Forrest Gump*

One weekend, late in the spring, I drove down to Orange County to visit my girlfriend and avoid my parents. If I ever had to be home, I would hole up in my room and listen to sermons. On that day, I remember texting Bryce and asking him to pray for me. I didn't know why; I just felt like I needed some cover fire.

So I was sitting there, on the little blue futon in my childhood bedroom, the one where I'd edited *Sierra Street* and written *Farmer's Tan*. The futon where I'd thought about God, but mostly about girls, and I opened my laptop computer. For the same reason we all like concerts, I enjoyed seeing pastors preach live. I wasn't the biggest fan of simulcast preaching, let alone laptop podcasts, but I really related to this one preacher, Mark Driscoll, from a church up in Seattle.

I liked Mark because he felt like a father to me. The kind you could ask any question and he would give you an answer worth regurgitating. I could also see the brokenness he carried beneath all the bravado.

So I came across this sermon, and it had a pretty unassuming title: "What Did Jesus Accomplish on the Cross?"[6] *Hmmm,* I thought, *I'll give it a whirl.* It was part of the Vintage Jesus series, and Mark was wearing a shirt that read, "Body Piercing Saved My Life." I guessed this referred to the nails through Jesus's hands, and I was tempted to think this shirt shouldn't exist. Personally, I preferred when Mark wore the shirt that read, "Jesus Saves," with a goalkeeper catching a soccer ball.

Mark began, "If John's gospel were a film, it would move fairly quickly through Jesus's life, and then the camera would pan in and everything would slow down and there would be an intense focus on the final week of Jesus's life as the cross is approaching as that being the culminating aspect of His life and His ministry on the earth."

"Good, he's talking about movies already," I chortled to myself. "This sermon is meant for me."

"My fear is that some of us may be so familiar with the cross that we sort of just pass it over—Jesus loves you and died on the cross for your sins—which is true, but sometimes the significance and the horror of that can be missed."

I started feeling like this sermon was *actually* meant for me.

"Now to explain crucifixion is probably going to shock you," he continued. "I'll just tell you as we get into it that someone at the nine [the morning service] passed out and someone at the eleven puked. Which I consider a very good sermon," added Mark with a smirk.

Without looking down at his notes, he started talking about scourging. The whipping that had occured before the cross. Mark described in bloody detail how Roman soldiers flogged Jesus with a cat o' nine tails—a whip with leather straps and metal hooks, basically a cord with claws that gathers into a man's flesh and pulls it apart. After making Him carry His own rough-hewn cross up the mountain, splinters eating into His open skin, the Romans then fastened him onto it, anticipating how His body weight would soon cause Him to slouch and suffocate on vomit, blood, sweat, and tears.

I didn't even know pastors could say stuff like this.

"If you saw the movie *The Passion of the Christ,*" Mark explained, "this was actually very accurately portrayed."

I had seen *The Passion* over a year before this. I didn't cry. In fact, I didn't really cry in movies ever. I was usually too busy critiquing them.

Quoting the book of Isaiah, Mark referred to Jesus on the cross as "one from whom people hide their faces … marred beyond human likeness." My mind rocketed to Eun-man, the boy on his back, the one I hid my face from for most of the shoot. I wasn't the only one to do that. Pastor Lee even did so when the boy was born. I wondered what Jesus looked like caked in blood and shredded. I remembered the iconography from the stations of the cross etchings from Catholic Mass. The crown of thorns, the robe, the holes in His hands.

Before this, though, I honestly thought people who were crucified just starved or froze to death up there. The way they hung, I never considered how they couldn't breathe. It reminded me of the kids in The Happy Room, choking on spittle and phlegm.

To button up his point, Mark quoted satirist Lenny Bruce: "If Jesus had been killed twenty years ago, Catholic schoolchildren would be wearing little electric chairs around their necks instead of crosses." My mind started reeling, and I felt so naive for wearing that cross like some Jesus Junk fashion statement.

In a relatable moment, Mark recalled first hearing about the crucifixion, and how he couldn't see this event as "good news" at all. I agreed. To me, it sounded more like a grisly tabloid, a headline about a criminal on death row, followed by excessive descriptions of his execution. But Mark then made a point of saying that Jesus wasn't only innocent but sinless. That He was the only sinless man who ever lived. A perfectly innocent man, sentenced to a perfectly wicked man's death.

I immediately began defining sin in my head.

Sin:
- Murder
- Lying
- Stealing
- Abuse
- Hitler
- Drinking and driving
- Drugs
- Adultery

I'd heard that Jesus came to die for my sins. I'd read this on coffee cups and signs that people hold outside the USC Coliseum, but I didn't feel like I was that bad. I didn't feel like I had done anything out of the ordinary. I didn't kill anybody. I had never cheated on my girlfriend. But then Mark said something no one had ever said to me before: "It's not just what you do; it's why you do it. Words count, deeds count, motives count, and [he paused dramatically] so do thoughts and longings of the heart."

Hearing this, I realized I was chewing my cheek like bubble gum, and that my stomach was knotting up. My paradigm of what sin was suddenly exploded, once again, "like fabulous yellow roman candles ... like spiders across the stars."[7] The Rolodex in my mind spun, and I saw dozens of pictures of girls I wasn't dating.

"Next thing you need to know is that the result of sin is death," he declared.

I started to feel sick, the kind of sick that pins you to the floor. I felt like I did back home with my girlfriend, when the guilt first set in.

"If it wasn't for sin," Mark said, "we wouldn't have funerals, we wouldn't have mortuaries, we wouldn't have cemeteries, we wouldn't have hospitals, we wouldn't have obituaries, we wouldn't have sickness and disease and war and famine and plague and death."

And maybe without sin, I wouldn't feel like this either. Without sin, maybe I wouldn't feel like dying because of my dirty thoughts; without sin maybe my dad and I would say "I love you" more often; without sin maybe my brother and I would have played together like the drawings he did; without sin maybe kids wouldn't be left in Dumpsters; without sin maybe actors wouldn't commit suicide; maybe my grandma wouldn't have gotten Alzheimer's and Colin's mom wouldn't have died and Hannah wouldn't have to be buried under the Christmas tree.

I remembered how some people said it was someone's sin that made Eun-man look the way he does. I remembered that Pastor Lee even asked God if there was something he did wrong, something that caused his son to come out all tangled up. I know now that God didn't curse Eun-man. But back then I asked Him that question too. The main difference was, my girlfriend was starting to feel like my version of Eun-man. My girlfriend was starting to feel like the one my sin tangled up.

"God made him who had no sin to be sin for us, so that in him we might become the righteousness of God,"[8] Mark said, quoting a Bible verse from some chapter I didn't know.

If you're a pedophile, Jesus became, on the cross, a pedophile. If you're an alcoholic, Jesus became an alcoholic. Even though Jesus didn't actually do any of those things, He got punished like He had been the worst of all those things. A liar, cheater, murderer, thief, coveter, pervert, and probably a porn addict too.

In my head, I started imagining Jesus taking my place throughout my whole life. Everything I ever did wrong, everything I was too ashamed to tell anyone about. I pictured Jesus with my computer on His lap, pants around His ankles. I pictured Him in bed, in a pink bedroom, cussing out a girl for not being enough. It was like a trial where Jesus got up and confessed to all the things I'd ever done, and I got to go free.

Sitting on my blue futon, in my childhood bedroom, listening to this on the same computer where I got caught looking at dirty videos, I cried like I never had before.

"Jesus lived the life I could never live, and Jesus died the death I should have died," Mark concluded. "Jesus went to the cross for me … and then three days later Jesus rose again because death could not hold Him…. That's why it's good news."

□

My grandma never had a funeral when she died. The only one I'd been to at this point was for an old friend named Sam. He was one of my best pals growing up, and he got lost along the way, just like me. I hadn't seen Sam in probably four or five years when I heard about him passing away, but one thing was certain: I wasn't missing his funeral. That's what you do for people you know and love. It sucked when Heath Ledger died in his hotel room, but I wasn't going to skip class for his memorial service. The thing is, when you really know somebody who dies, it doesn't matter what else you have going on. You get there. Whatever it takes. You get to that funeral.

So before I heard that He took my place, I knew a lot about Jesus. I knew a lot about His teachings and His values and His biography. But I didn't know Him. Not well enough to be at His funeral.

Now on my knees, not even checking the door to make sure no one was eavesdropping, all I could muster was a meager but real "I'm sorry." I kept saying that. "I'm sorry, I'm sorry, I'm sorry, I'm sorry." I felt like I had just run over a little boy. An innocent little boy. I hated myself for that.

Yet, even as I hated myself in ways I never had, somehow I was also the most loved I had ever been. Hearing that sermon wasn't the first time I felt guilty and ashamed for hurting people. It wasn't the first time I'd heard about Jesus. But it was the first time I admitted to cheating on my girlfriend. It was the first time I realized that who I was inside mattered. Even after giving my body away so many times, it was the first time I felt completely, desperately, and beautifully known.

It was like a mini-divorce when I broke up with my girlfriend, and it was ironic because I felt like I was abandoning her after I'd just finished making a film about abandonment. But I knew it was the best thing for her. I knew it was part of getting free, for both of us. Weirdly, I knew it was the most truly loving thing I'd ever do for her.

In South Korea I had spent several nights sleeping next to that box, waiting for someone to drop off a child, and no one ever did. But I did watch all of those videos, the ones Young showed us on her desktop. I had felt pity for those children, some of them deaf, some missing hands or even parts of their brain. But on the day I watched Mark Driscoll's sermon, I finally knew why Will couldn't take his eyes off that box back then. Why he couldn't look away from the little wooden womb. It was the first time I realized why God wanted me to meet Eun-man, the child who couldn't offer anything to anybody except problems.

For the first time in my life, I realized I was just one of those kids too, with nothing to offer a perfect God except my sin.

I was a broken child, bound up in the dark and then suddenly pulled out through the laundry room, by a Father, into the light.

Chapter 14

---

# HE COULD JUST GIVE

*Whatever you end up doing, love it. The way you loved*
*the projection booth when you were a little squirt.*

Alfredo, *Cinema Paradiso*

After cobbling together a cut of the film, I showed it to a few of my friends—including Sam, Bryce, and Will—and the reaction was thoroughly "meh." Unlike my old heart, the film lacked darkness, which makes for conflictedness, which is what makes life and stories interesting. Stuck in my brain like a harsh rebuke was Frank Capra's all-too-appropriate saying, "There are no rules in filmmaking. Only sins. And the cardinal sin is dullness." Altogether, my movie was a dull collection of cute baby shots, which would have been fine, if not for the recent documentary *Babies*, which was quite literally a collection of cute baby shots.

More to the point, I had a handle on what the movie was about on a surface level (man builds a mailbox for babies), but remained thoroughly uncertain about any deeper meaning. It was clear at this juncture, of course, that the movie was no longer mine. In the same way He was transforming me, God was also making this movie into a new creature. While watching it, I found myself getting more emotional than I ever had, even in scenes that used to make me shrug. I wanted the new cut of the movie to be about God, at least in some way. I didn't really understand how that could be done without seeming fanatical or forced, but I did know that my Korean plastic surgery angle needed to die.

"If only I could write the script for this movie!" I fumed. "If only I could just write something out for Pastor Lee to say, that would save us years! Gahhhhhhhhhhhhhhh."

For inspiration, I started watching lots of so-called "Christian films." Netflix has a genre tab for Faith and Spirituality, so I combed through those for anything that resembled the authentic experience I had while making my own film. I blew through the list in a couple of weeks, circumventing only the "Jesus meets apocalyptic action thriller meets Kirk Cameron" subgenre. Each film affected me, like a bad love song affects a middle school boy who has just asked a girl out on AIM. But rarely did the films capture what I saw in real life.

It seemed evident that the internal experience of conversion was almost impossible to externalize on-screen.

As I watched, all the Christian characters felt like they were in an AllState® Insurance commercial. "Are you in God's hands?" But as much as I wanted to correct other Christian filmmakers for turning their people into plot devices, the characters in my movie felt just as fake. There were diamonds in the rough, but overall, Pastor Lee looked uncomfortable on camera, like he was being asked all the wrong questions.

Palm firmly planted on my forehead, the only thing I knew for sure was that if we wanted to fix this issue, we were going to have to go back to South Korea. We didn't have any cash to burn, but just like the first time, I knew these convictions were bigger than me. Now knowing that life was more than movies, and knowing Jesus Christ for real, I refused to show the world a picture of Him that was anything less than the most authentic and beautiful picture I could create.

So I picked up the phone, and by the time I put it down, we had twenty thousand dollars coming down the wire and a whole new movie waiting for us across the world.

☐

Arriving in Seoul, I couldn't wait to walk up those steps and see Pastor Lee. It felt like a thousand years since I was there. On the ride over from the airport, I knew the movie was changing right before my eyes. It was no longer about Korean culture, plastic surgery, or perfectionism, as I had once planned it to be. Later on I would often say, "This movie is about all the things I didn't believe beforehand."

When I started making this movie, I did everything I could to stay out of sight, out of mind. I never wanted to be in the movie. I didn't want to be the punk from Orange County who flew to South Korea to solve all their complex domestic problems. I didn't aspire to be the intrepid Michael Moore/Morgan Spurlock host, talking to the camera and narrating the transitional scenes. I just wanted to tell the story and go home for a good shower. But as I stepped into the scenes I had been editing for months, I knew beyond a shadow of a doubt that I was in the movie. That I was in every scene the kids were in. And that, somehow, those former plot devices were now my favorite people in the world.

As I rode the roller-coaster cab up the same busy street, my head wasn't on a swivel, searching for angles this time around. Slinking through people traffic, I wasn't devising plans for the next crane shot or interview location. I was just peeking at the fish sunk into the ice at the markets and the sweet potatoes coming out in tinfoil from big black ovens. I was looking at the street doughnuts, packed with cinnamon butter, and the Korean grandmas with gentle faces sitting on blue benches and watching grandchildren all over the swings.

My heart wasn't in my throat this time. I halted the driver, nodded to Shayan, and smiled out the words, "We're back."

As we reached the front gate, we didn't even have to knock. They'd seen us pull up from the windows upstairs. Young was the first to welcome us, skirted by a few curious kiddies, barefoot in the thick August air. My new translator, Sooj Park, complete with a USC ball cap, embraced me on the stoop, ready and willing to translate all the things God had done in my heart since December. The kinds of things Pastor Lee would get most excited about. Standing behind Sooj, almost unsure if we'd remember him, was Ruri, wearing the cross I gave him.

He tugged at it and fiddled with the string, almost like he was trying to direct my attention to the present he hadn't taken off in eight months. "He says he missed you," translated Sooj, lifting up his cap to let heat out from under it. I hugged Ruri and said his name a few times to make sure he knew I hadn't forgotten and never would.

Climbing the steep stairs just inside the sliding door, Pastor Lee turned the corner and saw me. His eyes got big and he reached out his hand, first to shake mine, as if to say "Well done" and second to pull me into his chest. Then, appearing somewhat self-conscious, he ran his fingers through his hair, asking me if I liked his new haircut. I lied and said, "It's amazing." Somehow I felt like I actually understood what the Bible means when it says the word Father.

Once upstairs, Ju-eun (my new roommate) zigzagged into the room, squinting without his glasses and yelling "Hello!" at the top of his lungs. Pyong-gang (the boy with no right hand but capable of anything) practiced his kicks on my shins. Ga-ul (the beautiful baby who was named after the season she arrived—Autumn) danced around in her wavy skirt, and Gi-ri (the one who overcame heart surgery and is now known as Victory) somehow slept through all of this underneath the dinner table. It felt like the place God had in mind for His children to be.

I looked at Sooj and just laughed from a really deep place.

The next morning, they prepared fried eggs and English muffins, and each time Shayan and I would eat, the whole family gathered around like they were making sure the meal was American enough for me. After breakfast, we loaded the vans and drove the children to a large public water park. About halfway through the day, I put the camera away and waded into the shallow end with all my work clothes on.

Back at the house, Shayan and I lived on the orphanage floor (more accurately the puzzle-piece carpet on top of the floor), instead of the apartment down the road. We were in their world night and day, getting sick when the kids got sick. I "slept" next to Ju-eun, the boy who was aborted at seven months but survived. I put the word *slept* in quotations because Ju-eun kicked in his sleep like Landon Donovan, so I didn't actually get much shut-eye. But despite all that, I ended up holding him close to me each night, as though he were a baby brother or even a son.

Mark Twain once said, "Life would be infinitely happier if we could only be born at the age of eighty and gradually approach eighteen." I don't think Mark Twain knew Jesus, but when I read this, I felt like he was giving language to my feelings.

In so many ways, while living with the kids 24/7, I felt younger. And by that I mean I felt carefree and unbridled, even though it was like starting from scratch with some things, especially with the Bible. Each morning I was playing catch-up, just trying to learn everything I could about being a son of God. As I did, things that meant nothing to me before started to mean everything, especially the way Pastor Lee acted toward me. The way he fathered me.

As C. S. Lewis once said, "The sweetest thing in all my life has been the longing—to reach the Mountain, to find the place where all the beauty came from—my country, the place where I ought to have been born. Do you think it all meant nothing, all the longing? The longing for home? For indeed it now feels not like going, but like going back."[9]

It goes without saying that I didn't know a lot of theology, even theology around what I experienced. If you would have asked me at the time, I couldn't have explained penal substitutionary atonement, propitiation, or expiation. I couldn't have walked you through the doctrines of justification, regeneration, or sanctification. All I had was what God did for me. And that was enough.

Because whenever I experienced the love of God that summer, I started to tap into how Pastor Lee did it. How he did what I couldn't understand from the first time I read the article. How he adopted wildly difficult kids and how he was able to do it without losing his mind in the process. How he loved so courageously and went to the box every time the bell rang.

Pastor Lee's source of energy was so full that he could pour out without losing a drop. It was almost like there was constantly something being poured in. Like he was standing underneath the supply. I copied how he prayed on those summer mornings. And when the kids would start to get frustrating again, I'd pray with Pastor Lee, on my knees and out loud. What I found out is that you can love only as much as you are experiencing love. That's why Pastor Lee could love those who weren't outwardly beautiful, mobile, or able to speak. He didn't need anything from them. He had everything. He could just give.

Then, one morning, a miracle happened.

For a few days, Pastor Lee and his wife had been taking us to potential new home sites. We made use of this time by interviewing them on the way about when they first said "I love you."

On Wednesday morning, Shayan was prepping all the gear for our daily jaunt. We all knew Wednesday marked a really important day of traveling but for some reason, I just felt like we couldn't go. Sarah asked me why I was feeling this deep need to be at the house all day, but I couldn't fully explain it. Just like I couldn't explain why I needed to go to South Korea in the first place.

So Shayan and I started filming around the house, and I never second-guessed the decision.

Pastor Lee and his wife waved good-bye and shoved off and Sarah went downstairs to tend to the babies. Meanwhile, Shayan and I filmed the kids near the kitchen where the alarm bell was. We were watching Pyong-gang and Ju-eun play when suddenly, without warning, the alarm sounded. Everything went into slow-motion. Pastor Lee wasn't there, so no one really knew what to do. His wife also wasn't there so really, seriously, no one knew what to do. Shayan and I stopped filming and turned to one another. There were plenty of little scamps who could have gotten into the box, especially without Pastor Lee's supervision downstairs, and we'd had only false alarms in the previous twenty-five days of shooting.

But then somebody yelled out, "Baby box! Baby box!" And we both just bolted. Shayan fumbled to find the audio mixer, and I barrelled down the stairs to the box. Mrs. Lee's sister (her twin sister, by the way) paced across the carpet, praying that it was all a dream. With a little prompting, she agreed to inspect the box and opened it slowly, painfully slow.

As the wooden door creaked open, we saw a little white wrap, and inside that, a little red face. It was the middle of the afternoon and someone had just left a child forever. It was a sad moment, but the rush carried us out of the laundry room without time for it to feel tragic. We followed Mrs. Lee's sister up the stairs and she laid the baby on a blanket. I set my camera in front of the baby's face, trying to get all the footage I could before the police arrived. The baby didn't make a sound. Not a cry, not a whimper.

This was the first time, based on the videos I had seen, that the baby didn't even react. Then suddenly, just seconds after I pressed Record, the baby smiled. It was the kind of smile that stops parents from arguing over petty things. I didn't even know babies were able to smile at that age. But he did. He smiled like he was made to.

Now, in a moment like that, I wasn't sure how this child was going to grow up. I didn't know if he'd be adopted right away, after a long time, or at all. But I did know he and I weren't that different. Because I was an orphan once. Even with nice parents and a nice house, I was an orphan in my heart. I was begging for people to love me, to approve of me, to want me. And what I learned is that when you're an orphan, even just in your heart, you can love only those who will love you back. You can love only those people who have something to offer or who can reciprocate your feelings.

But as a child of God, you can be completely alone and still love people who have abandoned you. As a child of God, you can go to the people who have nothing to offer and give them all of you like Jesus did for all of us.

That's what that smile means to me now.

It means that we're all orphans until we know how much we're loved.

So, yeah, I became a Christian while making a movie. And that's funny to me because before that, movies were God to me. They were everything. Just like success or fame or security is to other people.

And I met this Korean man named Pastor Lee, who loved people with a love that just didn't compute with me at first. When we met, the only English words he knew were "coffee" and "I love you," but his life still spoke volumes into my own on that first trip. He was a dad, like the one I was reading about in the Bible, and he made disabled children feel like marathoners.

If I'm honest, I have to admit that when I went to meet this man in South Korea, I thought I was there to save a bunch of helpless kids. But the funny thing about God is He is always the Savior. Because when it comes down to it, we're all the ones who need to be saved.

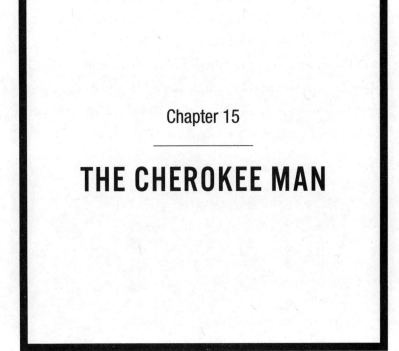

Chapter 15

# THE CHEROKEE MAN

*Your heart is free. Have the courage to follow it.*

Malcolm Wallace, *Braveheart*

In the fall, on my twenty-second birthday, my friends baptized me in a fountain.

The fountain was, of course, located in the same place where I told Will and Bryce about the drop box idea back in 2011. It was a pretty full-circle moment, as we stood right where I had refused to go years before, to the grassy lawn where mediocre musicians would play unplugged Christian alt music and everyone would all hold hands. My brother was there too, filming on his phone.

But nothing, absolutely nothing, about this was corny to me.

I've heard it explained that having a jersey doesn't make you a member of the team. You're still a member of the team even when you're not wearing the jersey, per se. Baptism is a little bit like the jersey—a statement to the church and to others that I now belong to the Man who "became me on the cross," that my old self was buried with Him (immersed in the water), and that I've also risen again as a totally new guy.

As a quick tip to anyone who gets baptized after reading this book, don't wear a white T-shirt just to impress girls who might be there. I'm not saying that's what I did, but just don't do it, okay? You'll regret it and write about it in a memoir one day.

Ankles under recycled fountain water, my new roommate and friend, David Beylik, started speaking to the group as people rode by on bicycles and made weird faces at what was about to go down on campus. David had come into my life recently and helped me understand what it meant to walk as a son of God more than anyone else. He also led a revival in his backyard when he was in high school and dunked a lot of ex–porn addicts in his pool, so I figured he was the man for the job.

"Everybody loves the new Brian," proclaimed David, and the crowd went wild. I think in years previous, I might have been offended by that statement. I might have wondered why people weren't in love with the old me. It was the first time I'd heard anything like that, and honestly, I wasn't offended … and I agreed with him. I liked the new Brian too. Standing in that fountain, for the first time in my life, more than my behavior was different. My heart was different, my deepest desires were different, and my brokenness didn't leave me crying on the floor.

James Jordan, a mentor from afar, explains it like this: "Now, just imagine for a moment. Now, this is stupid, all right? It's impossible and it's silly, but it illustrates a point. Imagine for a moment that you got filled with the spirit of Jim Carrey. If his spirit suddenly was in you, you might find your face pulling expressions it's never pulled before, right? It's like suddenly people would start laughing at you and your whole behavior, and you'd find an incredible ability perhaps to mimic other people and pretend to be other people like you never had before. You see what He's done? God has given us His spirit.… In other words, God has put His personality into us."[10]

Like James says, the change in me was from the inside out, and now I'm actually different. I am "Jim Carrey different."

"Today, this is the life I'm gonna live," I told the crowd, shirt now totally transparent. "I want people to know I love Jesus."

A few minutes later, this guy named Andy rolled by on a bike, wearing prescription Ray-Bans. David invited anyone else who might want to get dunked to step up, and Andy stopped and squeezed through to the front. I had never met him before. David and I baptized Andy in the same fountain, and I hugged him for a few minutes, once again reminded that even my baptism wasn't about me.

□

Later that fall, after submitting the latest cut of the film to Sundance, Sarah invited me to travel to Chad with a bunch of Korean humanitarians. After praying about it for ten to fifteen seconds, I decided to skip class and go. Right before Thanksgiving, we flew over with a small team to film a documentary on clean water initiatives. When we made our descent into Chad, there was zero ambient light. It was like we were making an emergency landing somewhere. The airport was overrun by beetles and I was let into the country without a visa. Stepping onto the bus, I quickly realized that everyone in or around the airport owned an AK-47 and that I was technically an illegal immigrant.

Through the darkest night I had ever seen, our hosts bused us to a janky hideaway called Hotel Shanghai, which had air-conditioning, turndown service, and more AK-47s. As comforting as my military safehouse was, I preferred the nights when we went out to the desert and camped in abandoned buildings. Lying next to a mosquito coil burner, with my camera tucked inside my jacket, I thought about the judges at Sundance sitting in plush red theater seats and watching our movie about God's love.

"Judges love cute babies. Judges aren't so hot for God. The movie isn't that good." My morale ebbed and flowed. Back at Hotel Shanghai, I got a personal message from a prominent film friend, which read, "Hey, I heard your film made it to Sundance."

"WHATTTTTTTT?"

I nearly keeled over and immediately summoned Sarah into my room to read the message. She was a little more skeptical. Of course, without an international phone, I was doomed to wait seven full days to check my voice mail to find out if my friend was a presumptuous fool. While in Chad, I met a man named Hamdune Mustafa, who said he converted to Christianity after realizing that the Quran is "a book written by man" but the Bible is "a book written by God." I told him my story too, the one about the box and the babies and the boy who got saved. On the plane home, I prayed and thought it all out. *It makes sense that we got in. We went back and made the movie God wanted us to make. It's His movie now and He's going to redeem my original intentions.*

As soon as we landed, I pressed down on the top button of my iPhone 4, waiting in agony for the little white wispy apple to materialize. After a zillion years, it finally did, and the phone booted up and blew up with texts and phone calls, as I had suspected. This was good. This was really good.

Checking my missed calls roster, I saw I had several calls from numbers I didn't recognize, any of which could have been Sundance admissions. The well-known protocol for Sundance admittance is "a phone call if you're in, an email if you're out." I didn't have any emails from them; I'd known that the whole week. But I'd been off the grid otherwise. I felt bad that they had been trying so hard to connect with me. I let everyone deplane before me, ear crushed against my weak iPhone speaker.

Checking each message one by one, I soon realized that my bank was looking for me and so was an old friend from New Mexico. But no one from Park City. A couple of weeks later, the official rejection email came in. I read it, deleted it, and didn't even kick anybody's dog. I didn't even yell.

For me, that was a much bigger deal.

■

While preparing the Sundance cut before going to Chad, I decided to watch all of Pastor Lee's interviews one last time, just to make sure I wasn't missing anything worth grafting in. I listened to Pastor Lee's story of how he used to get drunk after his second round and couldn't even get sober before meeting the girl who would later become his wife. I listened to the story of how Pastor Lee somehow won the girl back and took her home to meet his family for Chuseok (Korean Thanksgiving), and I again imagined it all in my head. I imagined Mrs. Lee sheepishly inching to the doorstep of Jong-rak's childhood home, and I laughed thinking of Jong-rak's parents swinging wide the front door, wearing hanboks, and saying something like, "The prodigal son returns!" I listened to Pastor Lee talk about how his older brothers yanked him into the kitchen that day and shamed him for bringing home such "a tiny woman," and how they later held down her hands and tried to pour Baekju (liquor) down her throat. I laughed when Pastor Lee explained how she literally flipped the table over, like Jesus did in the temple, and how rumors started going around that "Jong-rak's woman may have been small, but she was assertive."

She still is.

Digging further, I watched Pastor Lee pantomime the time he put his boss in the hospital for three weeks, and how the next day he sat slumped over the counter of a crappy hole-in-the-wall bar, running his finger around the inside of an empty shot glass. I watched his eyes as he talked about seeing his wife in the far corner of the pub and going over to her to ask why she was in this dump and not at home with their daughter.

"I saw my wife coming from the back, walking weakly from the bar," he said in one of the first interviews. "She said she took a strong medication and didn't know she was pregnant. She said she went to the ob-gyn and they told her the medication could make the child disabled. So she had an abortion. That's why she looked that way."

My mind started whizzing to all the ugly things God was turning into good things. Who would have thought that the couple who aborted a potentially disabled baby would end up raising fifteen *definitely* disabled ones? In those moments, Pastor Lee became just as broken, weak, and needy as the kids he cared for.

"On Monday, when I went to work, a pastor came in and started preaching about St. Augustine," he said with a smile. "You see, Saint

Augustine was very violent and corrupt, but thanks to the prayer of Mother Monica, he became a saint. And when I heard that, I thought, 'Someone like me can also become like that if I believe in God!' My heart was burning. Like somebody sitting in front of a strong fire. At church, the pastor shared John 3 and I knew then that God loved me. That He had called me to be a child of heaven and to be loved. So, from then on, I received salvation.... It was about that time that I started praying for a son."

This time, I listened to his testimony, and I understood it. I understood the sin and the pain that comes from the sin and the freedom in letting Jesus take it.

Then I came to an interview from the most recent trip, the only interview of Pastor Lee in a church.

"The reason I became their father was," explained Pastor Lee against some stained-glass windows, "God adopted me."

My heart stopped.

"That's it," I exclaimed. "That's the end of our movie."

■

In San Antonio, Texas, there's this festival they call "the Christian Oscars."

Otherwise known as the San Antonio Independent Christian Film Festival, these guys give out the largest cash prize for a winning film in the entire world:

$101,000, out the door.

Because our film was now more about God, and mostly because the prize money was enormous, we submitted the film to the Christian Oscars around the time we submitted to Sundance, in hopes that we'd just get in and get the rough cut in front of an audience of believers.

A day or two after I received the email from Sundance saying (basically) that our film sucked compared to the other films submitted, I got an email from San Antonio saying our film was amazing compared to every film ever! Okay, so the festival wasn't that enthusiastic, but they did offer us a boilerplate "Congratulations! Come if you can."

Problem was, the period before the festival was another dark night of the soul for me. The movie was supposed to be done a year earlier, and I had a hard time seeing people who had written checks and supported the project. Everywhere I went, it seemed, people asked, "When is it going to be done?" I also felt like we'd spent all this time and money, and what did we really have to show for it? A trailer with a few thousand views? There were covers of Kesha songs done by eleven-year-old boys that had more views than that. Moreover, I hadn't helped the family in any significant way yet, and I hadn't really changed the world like I promised I would.

At the time, I was beginning a new relationship with a girl from USC. Her name was Amanda and she had become a Christian a couple of years before me. Her "Pastor Lee" was a girl named Kristy Pyke, who led a Bible study on sorority row. Amanda told me that God was the One who carried her out of a frat party, which sounded a lot like the dark box I got carried out of in South Korea. We connected like war vets who had been rescued from the same POW camp but didn't know we were imprisoned at the same time.

Dating Amanda felt kind of like going to South Korea the second time around. I knew what I did wrong the first time and was determined to make something entirely new.

Before she left for Budapest (to study abroad for four months), Amanda kindly mandated that I be in San Antonio. Just in case something amazing happened. I took her to the airport with her family and kissed her on the forehead, still unsure how she could look at me without looking at my past.

"Just be there," she said, smiling. "Trust me."

Per Amanda's suggestion, I went home and bought a round-trip ticket for Texas and pleaded with my friend Addison for a place to crash, secretly praying that he lived near the Alamo. Over Facebook, Addison offered his sister's room for the weekend, and I got Will to drop me at LAX for an early morning flight.

"I've never been to a film festival before," I confessed in the car.

"Probably something God was saving," he offered.

With my dad's old suitcase in tow, I walked past the curbside and up to the American Airlines station to check in.

"Hello, the last name is Ivie, I-V-I-E. I'm heading to San Antonio."

"Okay, Mr. Ivie, let's see. Oh, my."

My heart sank.

"What?!" I asked her indignantly, my mind racing to movies like *Meet the Parents*, where conversations like this only ended with someone getting tackled on the plane by an air marshal.

"Sir, this reservation is for next weekend."

"Excuse me?"

"Yes, sir. You purchased tickets for next weekend. See the dates, just there."

She pointed at my reservation on my own phone. I was dumbfounded. With a line forming behind me, I crumpled on the floor of the airport. I felt like I had just failed eighth-grade Geometry. I browsed my text conversations for people to share these feelings with. God was not on my mind. I was too angry to pray. I was too frustrated to ask the God of the universe to help me find a flight.

With my head back against the wall, I decided to call my dad and explain what I'd done wrong. But before I could even get to the part about feeling stupid, he just said, "Use my credit card."

"What?" I replied.

"Use my card. It's for emergencies," he insisted.

And with that, I was on my way to Texas, on my dad's dime, telling him he could live stream the awards ceremony if he had a free evening.

Upon arrival, Addison's family asked me the odds of *The Drop Box* winning the documentary category. Without anything to back it up, I told them "really good," trying to better justify my intrusion into their lives. Plus, we still had the cute babies-meets-Jesus thing going for us, right? Heading over to the theater itself, I somehow missed both of my screenings but arrived in time to meet a Cherokee man sitting in a potted plant outside the auditorium, who smelled like alcohol the way I smelled like cologne.

I sat down and talked with him for a few hours. It brought me right back to how I used to interview people in South Korea. I asked him about his life, where he grew up, how his parents died, and how he ended up with a Heineken in a lunch bag outside of the Christian Oscars. At the end of the conversation, I felt like I'd come to Texas just to meet this man, and to call him by name. In six years of trying, this was the first film festival I'd ever been to. But God wanted me to skip it and have a conversation with somebody who was lost. At the end of our talk, I told my new friend that I'd wait for him tomorrow, but he never showed up at the River Walk again. As I shook his hand, the last thing he told me was, "No one shakes my hand. Not in a long time."

Sitting in the third row from the front on the far right side, I watched thousands gather in the hall. Doug, the festival founder, sang a song with his daughter, and they played theme music to *Jurassic Park*. Why not, right? Later in the evening, we won an award for Sanctity of Life, which was amazing, crazy, and something I didn't expect. Sitting there, I remembered my mom telling me a story once about how when she was pregnant with me, the doctor told her she could get screened to make sure I was a healthy baby. She refused, saying, "I'm having him either way."

After dozens of other awards got handed out, we finally reached the documentary film category, and I felt like we had this one in the bag. I sat up straight and cleared my throat, going through anecdotes in my head about the value of life, especially those lives the world devalues, like the Cherokee man in the potted plant.

In the middle of my thought, Doug announced the Documentary champion, and to my dismay, we lost to a movie made by another young dude, who looked like me in a few years. He seemed sincere, but I was still sad that I couldn't take that award home to my team. The next logical choice for Best of Festival was a movie about Nazi Germany, which was a highly professional narrative feature film that had already won Best Feature. Usually, whoever won that award also won Best of Festival. They went together, sort of like Best Drama at the Golden Globes and Best Picture at the Oscars go together most years.

In the midst of pin-drop silence, Doug leaned over the mic and performed a preamble on this year's winner.

"Well, ladies and gentlemen, it is now that time. Are you ready for the grand prize winner???"

The house went BANANAS with the kind of applause that even Doug's podium mic picked up really well.

"The 2013 SAICFF grand prize winner of $101,000 for Best of Festival goes to ..." You could hear him open the envelope in the microphone. As the sound scraped across the room, I leaned over to my buddy Jay and asked him if he'd seen the Nazi movie. Sitting there, whispering to Jay, I couldn't have been more thankful to have been a winner and to be taking home the Sanctity of Life award, which I actually felt like I understood—

"THE DROP BOX!" he exclaimed.

Immediately, the whole crowd stood around me, half of them unsure why a documentary on file sharing for businesses had won two awards that night.

I banked up the steps, looking at the upper levels of the theater the way Jim Hawkins looked up at the upper masts of his pirate ship. I was crying before I even got to Doug at the lectern. His kids were holding a huge check onstage. While I composed myself, Doug rolled the original Kickstarter video, the one I made at 4:00 a.m. the night before we posted it and where I said stuff like, "My name is Brian Ivie. I'm a student filmmaker from California, and this man [Pastor Lee] changed my life from six thousand miles away."

When I made that video, of course, I had no idea how true that would prove to be.

Doug was joined on the podium by R. C. Sproul Jr., who from the waist down looked like William Wallace (kilt) and from the waist up looked like General George Patton (military jacket, epaulets), and several other judges. I was still trying not to cry on television. "The man is a visionary," said one of the judges. "We've been challenging our young filmmakers to look at the 'Goliaths' that are out there and run to the battle. Many times we're moved with compassion but do nothing," acknowledged another.

"Your life is being purchased," Doug told me. Then he added, ironically, "Don't blow it. You're being given an investment. You are Jean Valjean at the beginning of *Les Misérables*, who got the candlesticks." I'd never read this book, but would later discover that Jean Valjean actually stole the candlesticks. When he comes back later after the police catch him, the priest doesn't press charges. Instead, he gives him more than candlesticks, and the police let him go free.

It was surreal, in a way, because I had already blown it, in so many ways these judges didn't yet know. And because of my humanity I knew I'd blow it again, but I also knew that God somehow makes the ugly things good again. Even dreams about winning film festivals and being famous.

"By His grace, the Lord brought Brian to Himself between trips because of what he saw in the Korean pastor. Real Christianity at work," said Geoff Botkin with a father's courage.

"When I grow up I want to be like that man [Pastor Lee]," proclaimed Stephen Kendrick to close out the judges' input.

*Me too,* I thought. *Me too.*

Finally I stepped behind the microphone. "Throughout my life I've been asked to speak a lot, and I always rely on my own cleverness," I quivered. "I honestly have to say that this is the first time it isn't prepared. I deified movies for twenty-one years of my life. I made it my idol and it failed me. I am done with that idol. I will steward this investment because I would rather tell the plainest truth with one hundred thousand dollars than the most sophisticated lie with a hundred million. I see Him [God] as a Father, and I see these kids as so indispensable. I'm just so grateful that I've been saved. I know that these kids who were saved in this box are going to change the world."

After winning the money, the first person I texted was Amanda.

She was on a train somewhere in Europe, without Wi-Fi, but when she found out, she sent a message back in all caps just to make sure I knew how proud she was of me, and also to make sure I remembered whose idea this San Antonio trip was in the first place.

When I started dating Amanda at USC, I was afraid of hurting her. Sometimes, in my sin, I just wanted to be locked up where I couldn't hurt anyone, especially another girl. But what I found out was that God doesn't show us our sin simply to reveal how awful we are. He shows us our sin so we can see there's a better way to make movies and love women. A better way to live.

And then He gives us new power to actually do it.

When I started to make this film, I did it for all the wrong reasons. I wanted to be famous. But God made that beautiful too. And with Amanda, God would go on to do some of the most redemptive work of my life. He would take a predator and make him a protector. A boy and make him a man.

As my pastor, Tim Chaddick, would say one Sunday, "You will have a heart for other people because in the gospel, you get a new one."

Two years later, the dirtiest site I've visited is YouTube. And by God's amazing grace, the only woman I've daydreamed about is Amanda.

Both the win in San Antonio and learning to love Amanda, even while she was on a train almost as far away as South Korea, taught me the same thing about God. That He's in the business of using weak, wretched people to do legitimately beautiful things.

And that many people can modify a sinner, but only God can make him into a saint.

Chapter 16

# FATHER'S DAY

*Therefore, if anyone is in Christ, he is a new creation.*
*The old has passed away; behold, the new has come.*

Paul, 2 Corinthians 5:17 ESV

After San Antonio, my parents demolished my childhood bedroom. In its place they built a guest room with butterflies all over it. When they first unveiled their handiwork one summer afternoon, I told them I would be needing a shrink to deal with my room becoming a little girl's room.

I don't live at home during the summers anymore, but Amanda and I have been going down to San Clemente lately so my parents know they're part of it. That they're part of our relationship, not just observing coyly over Facebook. I also utilize the time to Dumpster dive in their garage for items I plan to indefinitely borrow.

One morning, rummaging through the carcasses of my old life, I came across some old oil paintings in vintage wood frames. One was the face of a circus clown, the kind you'd see in a Tim Burton gallery. The other was an impressionist landscape where these old rusty brown cars were plowing through the snow beneath the California mountains. As a self-appointed hipster, I decided that these were the perfect additions to my alcove. They looked like originals too, which was a rare find for my parents' trash heap.

But underneath some of my old elementary school show-and-tells lay the best painting of all. It featured a hooded flutist playing gently amongst sheep, outside a foggy Jerusalem. There were three crosses in the distance too. It made me think of the guy who played cello in a bomb crater after the blitz in Sarajevo. The painting had both depth and innocence and was clearly the work of Matisse, Cézanne, or perhaps a young Banksy.

Holding the image close to my face, in the bottom right corner of the frame I saw a name: "Tommy." Probably some local painter from San Juan. *Bummer, but still worth some wall space*, I reasoned.

No, waaaaaait a minute. Not Tommy.

"T-O-M-I!" My mom painted these?

"Holy smokes!" I yelled.

Startled and incredulous, I sprinted into the house, brandishing the painting of Jerusalem, and demanded an explanation for the ostensible forgery. My mom giggled. "I painted that when I was thirteen," she said without blinking.

In that moment, I realized two things:

1. Tomi Tanabe was an alias.
2. I had undeniably inherited any and all artistic ability from my mom.

Up in LA, I nailed the painting to the wall by my bed. When I see it now, I remember to call home sometimes, and thank the woman who once insisted that quitting her job and staying home with me were the two best things that ever could have happened.

□

Not long after we got back from South Korea the first time, Kevin got into USC's School of Dramatic Arts. Everyone was stunned, but I wasn't. By pure mathematics, he wasn't supposed to get in, but as we all know, math is a complete waste of time (I quit math class my senior year). Plus, God made Kevin to perform, the way He makes other people to run.

Starting at USC, Kevin struggled to find his way at first, but then he joined CRU just like I did and even lived with Will's little brother, Christian, in the biggest party dorm on campus.

Nowadays, when Kevin and I make it home on the same weekend, we watch movies that we used to watch, the ones you rent before you get chest hair. Kevin still has none, of course. We make popcorn and pour Hershey's over Kirkland vanilla ice cream.

When Kevin was born, I didn't think he had any eyes because they were closed while I was holding him. I informed my mom that he needed some eyes. I must have loved my blind baby brother then, but for years I never told him. For some people that's probably no skin off their back, but for me, saying "I love you" to another guy in my family was like saying "Merry Christmas" to a guy named Marty Feldman or Josh Goldberg. I had always reserved those words for girlfriends and birthday cards.

But the summer after San Antonio, as Kevin was packing his car one weekend to go back to school, I remember saying, "I love you." Under his breath, he mumbled it back to me, avoiding eye contact either out of shellshock or to avoid smiling about it.

I tell him that I love him whenever I can now, and it's easy to.

The other day he told me he wanted to get baptized. Jumping out of my seat, I instantly told him what to say, what baptism symbolized, and which fountain on campus would be best for something of this magnitude, but he just politely texted back, "I was thinking of getting baptized in the ocean."

After a beat, I admitted that the ocean was a better idea and that Orange County was actually a beautiful place to celebrate.

Who would have thought, huh?

Around USC today, I'm better known as "Kevin Ivie's brother."

In film, you have to look really hard to find good portrayals of fathers. In most good movies, at least, the dad either actually dies, is dead emotionally, or is an abusive or (at best) emotionally estranged drunk. The moment of so-called reconciliation in these films tends to be one in which the young, transcendent main character just sort of makes peace with his father—it never really portends any actual hope for relationship. Most of the time, it's actually the father reaching out to the son for forgiveness. We see this in *Friday Night Lights*, as the abusive Charlie Billingsley character finally reaches out to reconcile with his son, Don, at the end of the film, and the son extends grace.

The true father figure in the film always ends up being the cool professor, the tough but loving high school football coach, the quirky uncle who tells cool stories and buys you beer, or the grandfather who gets you even though you're weird.

Sitting in the Jacuzzi tub on Father's Day, Dad and I raised glasses to each other. Over and over again, he told me how much he respected the work I was doing in South Korea and we talked about me being born again and what that was supposed to mean. We also drank beer and didn't talk about God at all.

Earlier that day, I stepped out of church with a heavy heart. I was feeling like I needed to talk to my dad about some of the ways he had hurt me in the past. No dad is short of failures, and I was convinced that Father's Day was the appropriate time to decipher what was between us and how we might become better friends or something. I felt nervous about unearthing past wrongs, but there was this weight on my chest like when you can't push the bench press on the last rep (I can use this analogy because I started working out to impress Amanda). I guess I just wanted it off.

Sloshing around in the bubbles that evening, I nursed my Hawaiian ale and my dad started asking me questions about Paul, the apostle. I told him how Paul used to go by Saul when he wanted Christians to die. I told my dad about Peter as well and how he was crucified upside down for the gospel's sake. Now on the subject of wounds, I racked my brain for just the right words to remove the blockage that had been killing us for the past decade. The hot tub was a strange context for this kind of thing. But there we were … Dad, big and weathered looking, and me looking and feeling as skinny and childlike and insignificant as ever. Then, like someone else was saying it—

"Dad, I'm sorry," I blurted out.

"Why are you sorry?" he asked with a genuine turning of the head.

"I've never honored you. For most of my life I've just ignored you. I know I did when I would stay out all night. I never listened to your advice about work or money or girls. I never gave you the chance to teach me anything. I just wanted to say I'm sorry for how I've treated you and Mom."

My dad's eyes widened like I was Juno admitting to a recent pregnancy.

As I tried to fill the silence again, he cut me off and started to say something classic and expected about how all kids have their rebellious time. How he knew I'd eventually come around and become a man. It occurred to me, then, that if I got my artistic acumen from my mom, I probably got my salesmanship from Dad. But I couldn't let him believe that. He had to understand that those words weren't from me.

"Without God," I told him, "I never would have apologized to you. I didn't want to. I didn't feel like I needed to. It just wasn't in me."

Dad nodded and wrapped a towel around his waist.

As he did, I poured my warm beer into the bushes and offered an awkward "I love you" and I meant it. After that, we didn't go skeet shooting or even out for his favorite food, but it ended up being the best Father's Day on record. I felt like a son to my dad the way Jesus was a Son to His Father. And that's still what I try to be—a true son, both to the father in the hot tub and the Father in heaven.

It took years of apologizing for me to find home again. But the relationship with my dad is different now. He stops by my office every month or so, and we like seeing movies about baseball. The other day, I even started writing a screenplay based on the true story of my dad and his friends in the 1970s, teaming up against evil.

After walking into the new guest room (my old room), I opened the sliding door to the closet, expecting to see my old VHS tapes with "Ivie" written in Sharpie on the spine. But all I found there were women's shoes. The carpet that couldn't be cleaned because of all the newspaper clippings piled up everywhere was now padre brown hardwood. The walls once coated with Rolling Stones albums and Woody Allen LaserDiscs were now a muted green color, and along with the butterflies there was a painting of a birdcage to the right of the big window.

Standing there against the threshold, watching the sun spill onto the down comforter with flowers all over it, I smiled at all the things God had done in my life and in my parents' house. At all the ugly things He turned into beautiful things and how He redeemed me from a life where the blinds were always closed on things I was ashamed of. All the screams that had become singing. All the silent meals that had become barbeques. All the closed doors that had become open ones.

These days, I watch fifties movies downstairs with my mom (like *Marty*) and play catch with my brother in the backyard. When I'm home, I ask Mom if she needs help with anything before I do my work, and I hug her even when I've been around her for hours already. Sitting at the table where I read about Pastor Lee back in 2011, I talk to my dad about investing and how to treat my car as an asset. I also tell him "I love you" when I leave to go to a normal place like the bank. I can't say it enough.

In the backyard, I play with our two new dogs, Calvin and Hobbes, and help tend to my mom's garden. On Sundays we even go to church together, not just twice a year, but whenever I'm home, and Amanda sleeps really well in the new guest bed. Her room, my old room, is really the most luminous place in the house.

Thinking of it now, seeing my old room as a new creation may not have meant much to the designer, and it may have been a little sad for my nostalgic mom, but to me it had become a garden. The kind you read about in the beginning of the Bible.

The kind Jesus walked through after He came back to life.

Epilogue

# THREE LETTERS

I remember being asked once why someone should ever become a Christian. And I think people ask because it's not always clear that life would be that different. Christians still fail and still fall apart at times. And from the movies and the media, Christian life doesn't even look real. It looks like the fakest thing on the planet.

But when I first met Christians, I met the most authentic and honest and joyful people I had ever met in my entire life. I didn't meet hypocrites. I met people who talked about their addictions and their crap. I met people who weren't afraid to be known.

Back in South Korea, when I would walk those streets late at night, hiding from people's opinions of me, I enjoyed not having to perform for others. When I was with pretty girls back in high school, I enjoyed just getting to be real and not having to prove myself. The difference with God is that I can be the same wherever I am. In a crowd or alone, I use the same language and struggle with the same issues. I'm like a little kid who isn't even capable of leading a double life because I'm fully known and fully loved.

Which is why, when I first met Christians like Will, Bryce, Sarah, Sam, and Pastor Lee, I felt like I was meeting children.

I felt like I was meeting sons and daughters, looking to fold laundry and help others as Ruri did, in a cold and orphaned world.

*Dear Pastor Lee,*

*Thank you for answering my email. Thank you for your response from the outset and for making sure it was never really about you or just about a movie. Thank you for saying, "Hey, you're welcome to come live at my house, and whatever happens, happens." Thank you for being up at all hours of the night … like me. You were up waiting for Eun-man to choke, but it was a comfort for me to know that you were still awake and were still there.*

*Pastor Lee, thank you for coming to the roof that night I was filming up there, in the middle of the night. I was standing on your kids' play table and I broke it. I fell right through it with a crash. Thank you for running up to the roof when you thought I was in trouble. I was, in a very real way, in trouble. Thank you for not ridiculing me but for giving me a thumbs-up and heading back to bed.*

*Thank you as well for how you look at me and react to me after I've been gone for a long time. You look at me like I've just returned from being gone at sea.*

*Pastor Lee, thank you for showing me your life before God, so I could finally understand where all the love came from. Where all the courage came from. Thank you for never taking the glory, even when you stay up all night and destroy your own body to save the cold, little ones that might be left outside.*

*And thank you for continuing to get up every time that bell rings.*

*Your spiritual son,*
*Brian*

*Dear Dad,*

*I'm sorry for being such a punk. For talking down to you and for not thinking you had anything to teach me about women, love, family, sacrifice, or God. I'm sorry for avoiding saying "I love you" when I left the house. I'm sorry for not being comfortable with that.*

*Thank you for wanting to go on the trip with me to South Korea. Thank you for wanting to go and protect Kevin and me from everything, from Kim Jong Il to catching a cold to not knowing how to hail a taxi. Thank you for driving me to your hometown to play a villain in my first movie. You were terrible, but if you had been good, it would have looked very out of place with the rest of the film.*

*Dad, thank you for loving it when you see me stop and rest. Thank you for loving Mom and for still holding her hand.*

*I know there were times, growing up, when I stormed out of the house and said I hated you and meant it. But now I love you, and I mean that more. I love you like I never thought I could.*

*Dad, when I was little I thought you could just leave work to hold the camera for me on my movies. I know now that it cost you a great deal. Thank you for selling things so that I could create things and for wanting my dream for me. More than you wanted to work for the Dodgers or live any of your dreams ... maybe even ones you haven't told me about.*

*I love you, Dad. And I always will.*

*Your son,*
*Brian*

*Dear God,*

*Thank You for sending Your Son to die for me. Thank You for bringing me back to life when I was dead in front of a computer screen. I'm sorry for treating people like characters in the movie of my life. I'm sorry for living for myself because that's one of the worst sins of all.*

*Making The Drop Box was the hardest thing I've ever done. I felt inadequate most of the time, like a complete failure other times, and at night wished it could just stop.*

*God, making this thing felt like being dragged behind a chariot. It felt like scales were being ripped off of me like what happened to the boy in The Voyage of the Dawn Treader. Making this movie went against all the childish things in me. It forced me to be considerate and take responsibility and respect people I didn't and always keep my promises. It forced me to grow up. It sorta felt like going to Neverland and becoming a pirate. Yet, I've also somehow become a child again. People think that means being naive and dumb, but I think it has a lot more to do with feeling helpless. It has a lot more to do with realizing just how weak and helpless I can be and how I need You even more than those children need Pastor Lee.*

*God, I still don't know a lot about pain or about death. But I do know that sin brought suffering into the world. And that Your suffering was the only thing that could take it out.*

*In the end, maybe I always liked battles because that's where you were. In the fog. In the thick of it.*

*Because real life isn't found watching movies. It's found fighting for others. The way You did on the cross for lost people like me.*

*Your son forever,*
*Brian*

# GET INVOLVED

*To donate or get involved with Pastor Lee's*
*lifesaving ministry, please visit:*

www.KindredImage.org

## KINDRED'S MISSION

Kindred Image exists to support the vision and legacy of Pastor Jong-rak Lee and his flock.

## KINDRED'S PASSION

Kindred Image is a nonprofit organization that works to support the vision and legacy of a courageous pastor in South Korea. What began as a desperate one-man campaign to protect life in one small neighborhood is now an organized effort to love and serve mothers in crisis, and never see an abandoned child on the streets of South Korea again. For the rest of the world, Kindred hopes to restore the idea of a God-given "kindred image," thereby defending the dignity and value of all human lives.

## KINDRED'S MODEL
### PREVENTION

We want to put an end to abandonment. But we know that this is a matter of the heart. Through story-based awareness, we work to change cultural consciousness and change prevailing views of single mothers and children with disabilities.

## INTERVENTION

We never want to sit on the sidelines and simply tell stories about abandonment. Led by Pastor Lee's compassionate vision, Kindred staff members serve at the drop box site, where precious lives truly hang in the balance.

## RESTORATION

We know that crisis care alone isn't enough. Through counseling, care packages, and the building of a new facility for holistic care, we are committed to walking with mothers and children through difficult circumstances and into brighter futures.

# KINDRED'S ETHOS

- We believe everyone is made in the image of God and is, therefore, beloved, sacred, and precious.
- We believe Pastor Lee is a faithful father of the abandoned and protector of the least of these.
- We believe God is the ultimate Father, who graciously sent His only Son to save the broken and the lost.

*The fight for life is more than just political. In so many ways, it's decided in the cultural imagination—and heroes like this provide the inspiration we need to replace cultures that spawned Kermit Gosnell, sewer pipes, child abandonment, and forced abortions with a culture that looks more like the home of Pastor Jong-rak Lee. That, my friends, is overcoming evil with good.*

—John Stonestreet, *BreakPoint*

# NOTES

1. Steve Martin, Carl Gottlieb, and Michael Elias, *The Jerk,* directed by Carl Reiner (Beverly Hills, CA: Aspen Film Society, 1979).

2. Jack Kerouac, *On the Road* (New York: Viking, 1997), 254.

3. Kerouac, *On the Road,* 12.

4. John M. Glionna, "South Korean Pastor Tends an Unwanted Flock," *Los Angeles Times,* June 19, 2011, http://articles.latimes.com/2011/jun/19/world/la-fg-south-korea-orphans-20110620.

5. Lee Jong-rak, "Ju-sarang Community Church: A Place with Heaven's Comfort and Life," PowerPoint, slide 12.

6. Mark Driscoll, "What Did Jesus Accomplish on the Cross?" Vintage Jesus series (sermon, Mars Hill Church, Seattle, October 8, 2006), www.youtube.com/watch?v=L5d7fVOHqYU.

7. Kerouac, *On the Road,* 12.

8. 2 Corinthians 5:21.

9. C. S. Lewis, *Till We Have Faces: A Myth Retold* (Glasgow: Collins, Fount Paperbacks, 1981), 35.

10. James Jordan, Fatherheart Ministries (lecture, Vista Assembly of God, Vista, CA, March 15, 2014).